4.98
note
Quality Bks.
2/15

# The Book of
# GAMBLING

The Book o

Peter Arnold

# GAMBLING

Hamlyn
London·New York·Sydney·Toronto

Published by
The Hamlyn Publishing Group Limited
London · New York · Sydney · Toronto
Astronaut House, Feltham, Middlesex, England
© The Hamlyn Publishing Group Limited 1974

ISBN 0 600 39288 0

Filmset by London Filmsetters
Printed in Spain by
Printer Industria Gráfica sa, Tuset 19
Barcelona, San Vicente dels Horts, 1973
Depósito Legal B.35490–1973
Mohn Gordon Ltd. London

# Contents

## Chapter 1

# The Phenomenon of GAMBLING

What is gambling? It is to speculate on an uncertain event, involving the placing at risk of money or other possessions in the hope of achieving more money or better possessions. Nobody can avoid gambling since nobody can foretell the future. When marrying, one gambles one's happiness against the chance of greater happiness. Even to choose not to marry is to gamble that this will prove to be the better course. One gambles when buying shares or a motor-car. When making a car journey, or crossing the road, one stakes one's life or health on one's road-sense or agility. Insurance companies gamble with each policy. Of course, the gambling in the examples given consists of backing one's judgment or skill. Insurance companies rarely go bankrupt, because of the skill of their actuaries. In other gambles skill and judgment are irrelevant: these gambles might be called pure or true gambles. Betting on the toss of a coin is a true gamble. An amusing example of this form of gambling occurred in the film *The Sheep Has Five Legs*, when Fernandel and his shipmates bet on which of two cubes of sugar a fly would first alight upon. The fly's wanderings included a tour of a semi-clad young woman, instructed not to move. Incidentally, as crooks have devised ways to doctor sugar cubes, this gamble is not always as pure as it seems. For the purposes of this book, gambling is taken to mean the betting of money on events involving chance, or both chance and skills.

Gambling may not be a human need in the class of food, shelter or sex, but its practice is remarkably universal, and it is found in all societies and at all social levels. The ancient civilizations of Greece, Egypt and Rome had gambling equipment: dice, in the form of astragals or sheep-bones, counters and gaming boards or tables existed hundreds of years before the birth of Christ.

Why do people gamble? The Russian novelist Dostoevsky was a confirmed gambler; he wrote his novels under the pressure of mounting bills, and his gambling served to increase the pressure. Through the narrator of *The Gambler*, his partly biographical novel, Dostoevsky describes an initial depression at the sordidness of the casino, the oppressiveness of the crowd within, and the seriousness with which the gamblers concentrate on the spin of the wheel and the fate of their stakes. Forced into gambling by the need to make some money, he at first succeeds and describes the irrational feeling of power which winning induces. Later he encounters a losing run but nevertheless discovers a sense of infallibility, a certainty that he cannot continue to lose indefinitely. He bets recklessly and loses his entire capital. Dostoevsky then describes the overwhelming excitement provoked by the stupid loss of a large sum. It is

Feodor Dostoevsky, novelist and gambler

Jeanne Moreau plays a compulsive gambler in *La Baie des Anges*

The spoils: cashing the chips

perhaps this reaction which distinguishes the pathological gambler: the winning or losing becomes
subordinate to the thrill of gambling. The emotion
aroused by losing is as fascinating as that of winning.
The gambler in Dostoevsky's story retains his faith
in his infallibility and continues to gamble with
borrowed money in the certainty that he will
eventually win. Most people occasionally experience
this superstitious feeling of uniqueness, a belief that
natural mathematical laws do not apply to them. It is
a trait of the gambling addict that such an awareness
is allowed to colour his whole personality and he
risks everything on the basis of it.

There are various reasons why less committed
people gamble. Some may sound fanciful, and not all
apply to all gamblers. The main ones can be
itemized thus:

### 1. Greed
Perhaps the most basic and the least requiring
explanation. Easy unearned money has obvious
attractions. It is a prime motive of gamblers from
low income groups, with little skills and little
education, who see gambling as the one route to
wealth.

### 2. Snobbery
Gambling is regarded by some as a means to social
betterment or social admiration. Successes lead to
recognition by social superiors.

### 3. Alleviation of boredom
There is a strong inducement to gamble among
people of a low standard of living. It is an escape
to a sort of glamour from a depressing environment
or a dull routine job. It enables people to belong
to a group and to share a common interest or culture:
gambling has its jargon and its hard luck stories to
share with sympathisers. The betting shop and
casino are sources of company: in providing friends
with mutual interests they share the functions of
public houses or clubs.

### 4. Intellectual gratification
In games of skill, like certain card games, the
pleasure of playing well may be even greater than the
pleasure of winning money. The money won may
be merely the measure of the skill employed. To the
good bridge player, taking his friend's money may
even inspire guilt and detract from the satisfaction
of winning.

## 5. Belief in luck

Gamblers will rarely admit to being lucky, but many nevertheless gamble on the basis of a faith in their own good fortune. Extremists become pathological gamblers like Dostoevsky's character, firmly believing in their capacity personally to influence the vagaries of chance. Large numbers of less irrational people subscribe to the belief by backing lucky numbers or following private gambling rituals. All gamblers with these tendencies will be encouraged by recent work in the study of extra-sensory perception: learned psychologists can be found who will agree there is convincing evidence for precognition. Even more extraordinary are experiments which suggest some people have the faculty to 'will' certain unpredictable events, like the number which will appear on a die. Casinos often contain gamblers busily 'willing' certain events, but have found no necessity so far to ban them. Cynics might sympathize with Henry Labouchère, the English editor and wit, whose name is given to various gambling systems, and who said, 'I do not object to Gladstone's always having the ace of trumps up his sleeve, but only to him pretending that God put it there.'

## 6. Excitement

Jaded spirits can be given an uplift by a bout of gambling. To join the crowd at the races or around the roulette table, and to bet with them, is to join a group where ordinary existence is speeded up, however temporarily, by expectancy and tension. Triumphs and disasters are in the air. The gambler is where the action is, participating and making decisions.

## 7. Fantasy

Gambling provides opportunities to act a part: to be dominant or aggressive, to be stoical if losing, charming and magnanimous if winning. It offers a way of shedding frustrations or sublimating sexual drives. Some reckless gamblers are compensating for a repressed childhood or rebelling against a parsimonious upbringing. There is an element of masochism, perhaps, in those gamblers who think losing the next best thing to winning. It may go further than that in some, who appear actively to court financial punishment.

For a variety of reasons, the number of people who gamble and the total betting turnover cannot be estimated accurately. For a start, many gamblers will not admit to taking part, because they think it vaguely sinful. Secondly, some forms of gambling are illegal in various parts of the world and are carried on under cover. Thirdly, tax laws make for spurious gambling figures. Wins can be exaggerated, losses played down.

In rich Western societies, it is estimated that 90 per cent of adults have bet at one time or another, and about 10 per cent of these bet regularly. The scale ranges from those who bet only on the big horse-races of the year, through those who attend bingo sessions once a week, to those people, who might be classed as sick, who wear a gauntlet on one hand so that they can spend all day pulling the handles of two, three or four one-armed bandits, which they play simultaneously.

Annual gambling turnover in Western countries is frequently assessed by various methods. The assessments vary considerably, but usually have one thing in common: they are greater than the sums spent on education, hospitals, house-building, drink or tobacco. A figure for betting turnover, once assessed, is misleading, because the same money is bet over and over again. So the total turnover is much greater (about eight times greater) than the amount actually *spent*, or lost to the bookmaker or gambling proprietor. With these reservations, it is estimated that the amount of money being gambled in Britain annually in the 1970s is over £2,250 million. Of this, £900 million is bet on horses, £600 million in casinos, £300 million on bingo, £250 million on greyhounds, £175 million on football and £30 million on gambling machines.

In the United States, betting turnover is perhaps one hundred times higher than in Great Britain, several times higher than the turnover of the largest corporations, like General Motors. Nevada is the great gambling state, where most forms of gambling are legal. Most other states allow betting on horses on the race track itself, but off-track betting is illegal. However, illegal bookmakers flourish all over the United States, and illegal betting on horses is the largest gambling pastime. The policy, or numbers, game is illegal, but nevertheless the turnover probably tops $1,000 million.

In Australia, bookmakers are licensed and betting on horses is the most popular gamble. Bookmakers are becoming fewer as states prefer the totalizator system, particularly for off-course betting. The government has come to terms with gambling in Australia, and although some states ban some forms of gambling, all states run or license official lotteries. Lotteries are also licensed in New Zealand, where proceeds go to welfare. Betting on horses is legal in New Zealand through the totalizator agency, but some forms of gambling are illegal.

South Africa allows betting on race tracks, but other gambling is illegal. Japan allows government licensed lotteries, and betting on racing, whether the 'runners' are horses, boats or bicycles. Proceeds go to the government, who encourage particularly the horse-racing industry.

Eastern betting, with an ancient Chinese abacus as an aid to settling

Opposite: Roulette in an Egyptian casino.           Above: Bingo in a Great Yarmouth arcade

Many countries permit lotteries run or licensed by the state, where proceeds go to government schemes or charities, but nevertheless ban private gambling, either totally or in part. Canada and most South American countries, i.e. Brazil, Argentina, Bolivia, Mexico and Peru, are in this category.

An expert in advertising—and not a bad tipster either, it seems

Great Britain has very enlightened gambling laws. Most forms of gambling are allowed but regulated by strict licensing. Bookmakers, casinos, pools and raffles are permitted, if licensed, and the government runs a premium-bond savings scheme, where interest on deposits is distributed to bond holders on a lottery basis. A straightforward state lottery, while having many advocates, has so far been resisted.

France allows a few lotteries run for the state or

charity and a large *pari-mutuel* (tote) organization for betting on horses. Casinos and gambling clubs are also permitted, but bookmakers and most private gambling is illegal.

Scandinavian countries run state lotteries and football pools and allow on-track betting on horses. Private gambling is illegal.

West Germany and Italy have state lotteries, license casinos and allow betting on horses. Betting

shops are numerous in West Germany, and much of the proceeds of the lotteries and the tax on bookmakers is donated to sporting organizations, and no doubt accounts for this country's success in international sport.

Although gambling would seem to be anathema to Communist philosophy, representing the worst of capitalist diseases, the Communist countries have found lotteries and football pools to be good sources of revenue, much of which is used to sponsor sport. Private enterprise gambling is, of course, not allowed.

The reason much gambling is illegal is because it has become associated with crime. This is inevitable: where vast sums of money change hands on a basis of chance, cheating, confidence trickery, protection, bribery and corruption are sure to arise. Unfortunately for the proscribers, gambling is too popular to be stopped, and crooks will flourish in an illegal atmosphere. There are obvious parallels with American prohibition.

The naïve gambler is unaware of what goes on around him to part him from his cash. He does not suspect that fellow gamblers in casinos or fun fairs may be 'shills', or establishment employees paid to encourage him to gamble more, or that the horse he has backed may be doped, or that other players in a private game may be 'hustlers', skilled operators getting a living from social gambling gatherings, or that card sharps and dice mechanics exist, or that equipment might be rigged in the most expensive and scientific manner. He will not know that the ownership of casinos in Las Vegas has frequently been decided by ruthless gang warfare and that large sums have been paid to government officials and police chiefs for licences and protection.

Is gambling itself immoral? Gamblers would say that betting in moderation harms nobody, that it provides amusement, that all life is a gamble anyway and that, properly organized, gambling could provide revenue for the state and charities. Anti-gambling opinion would say that gambling in excess causes misery, both to the gambler and to his family, that moreover gambling even in moderation provides revenue for the underworld. President Kennedy was of the opinion that profits from gambling were directly financing corruption which was in turn directly undermining American society. Christians would argue that life is not a gamble and that the state and charities should not accept money won by individuals' misfortunes. These arguments are about the practical implications of gambling but do not answer the question of whether or not gambling is intrinsically immoral. Neither Roman Catholic nor Protestant churches express a firm opinion, and few churchmen state categorically that gambling is ethically wrong. Indeed church raffles are not unknown.

Gambling might be likened to drinking alcohol. In moderation it is enjoyable. It is a diverting pastime, particularly if it is shared with friends. If it becomes an obsession, it can destroy an individual and bring misery to his immediate circle. The majority of gamblers are not concerned with ethics. They will continue to make their bets, lose a little money, and consider it well spent.

# ARITHMETIC
## of Gambling

## Chapter 2

Mathematics is often thought to be dull and difficult, but a knowledge of one branch of it is necessary to gamblers. Indeed, nothing else more sorts out the serious gamblers from the mug punters. That branch is the one which deals with the theory of probabilities, and to the true gambler it can be fascinating. A knowledge of it will not guarantee a profit from betting, but it will cut out unnecessary losses.

The gambler needs to know about the calculation of odds, permutations and combinations, what constitutes a fair bet, how to spot the flaws in apparently impregnable systems, and how to calculate the percentage against him arising from a casino's or bookmaker's need to make a profit.

Most discussions of probability begin by looking at the possibilities which arise from tossing coins. It must be assumed, at the start, that if a coin is tossed fairly, the chances of it landing head or tail uppermost are equal. This need not necessarily be true, as the two sides of the coin are different and a physicist might one day be able to show that any coin is fractionally more likely to land on one side than the other. However, for the purposes of argument we must assume that 'heads' and 'tails' are even propositions.

The law of probability states:
The probability of any particular outcome to an event (provided that all outcomes are equally likely) is the proportion between the number of cases favourable to that outcome and the total number of cases possible.

In tossing a coin, there are only two possible outcomes, and if one desires a head, one outcome is favourable. Therefore the probability of a head is $\frac{1}{2}$.

An event, in gambling terms, is known as a 'coup', and the sum of all the probabilities in a coup will be 1. Let us verify this immediately. The only other possibility in one toss of a coin is a tail, and that also has a probability of $\frac{1}{2}$. The sum of the probabilities of a head or a tail is $\frac{1}{2} + \frac{1}{2} = 1$.

Let us now toss the coin twice and examine the probabilities in a series of two coups. The chance of the first spin being heads is $\frac{1}{2}$ and of the second being heads is $\frac{1}{2}$. To find the chance of both being heads we must multiply these two probabilities: $\frac{1}{2} \times \frac{1}{2} = \frac{1}{4}$, or 25 per cent, or one chance in four. The chance of first a head then a tail (abbreviated to HT) is also $\frac{1}{2} \times \frac{1}{2}$, or $\frac{1}{4}$. Similarly, the probability of TH is $\frac{1}{4}$, and of TT is $\frac{1}{4}$; therefore the sum of all chances is:

$$HH + HT + TH + TT = \frac{1}{4} + \frac{1}{4} + \frac{1}{4} + \frac{1}{4} = 1$$

It can be seen that the probability of two different results (HT or TH) is equal to the probability of the same result (HH or TT): both represent 50 per cent. This is true whether one coin is tossed twice or whether two coins are tossed simultaneously.

When tossing one coin, the number of possible results is two (H or T). When tossing two coins it is four (HH, HT, TH, TT). The number of different results possible for any number of coups can be expressed by the formula $A^n$, where A is the number of alternative results of a coup (in this case two: heads or tails) and $n$ is the number of coups. Thus for four spins of a coin, the possible results total $2^4$, or $2 \times 2 \times 2 \times 2 = 16$, for five spins $2^5$ or 32, for six spins $2^6$ or 64. The possible results for six spins are shown in Diagram 2:1.

It will be seen that in the diagram there is only one line of six heads. Therefore the probability of all six spins being heads is $\frac{1}{64}$, the same as for all being tails. There are six lines with one tail; therefore the probability of five heads is $\frac{6}{64}$, or $\frac{3}{32}$. The probability of a 5:1 distribution, with either heads or tails predominating, is $\frac{3}{32} + \frac{3}{32}$ (the *sum* of the two probabilities), or $\frac{3}{16}$. The probability of a 4:2 distribution is $\frac{15}{32}$, and the probability of 3 heads and 3 tails is $\frac{20}{64}$ or $\frac{5}{16}$.

Probability, then, is best expressed as a fraction. Thus, the probability of exactly three heads in six spins of a coin is $\frac{20}{64}$, which means there are 20 ways in which it can happen in a total of 64. When comparing many diverse probabilities it might be more convenient to convert the fractions to percentages: a probability of $\frac{20}{64}$ might be expressed as 31·25 per cent. When converting this probability to odds, one must deduct the 20 from the 64 to find the number of cases where exactly three heads will not happen; thus, the odds against exactly three heads in six spins are 44–20, or 11–5.

We can use this example to look at what the layman calls 'the law of averages', which undoubtedly causes the most misconceptions in gambling. Let us change the heads/tails alternative to boys/girls. Assuming that at each birth, the chances of a boy or girl being born are equal, and ignoring complications like identical twins, what are the chances of parents of six children having 3 boys and 3 girls? Many people believe that according to the law of averages it is likely. This is quite wrong. Our heads/tails calculations say that the probability is only $\frac{20}{64}$. It is $1\frac{1}{2}$ times more likely that the children will be four of one sex and two of the other: the probability of this is $\frac{30}{64}$. If one wants a balanced family, one should plan for two children, where the chance of having one of each sex is even. With four children, it is an even chance that there will be three of one sex, one of the other. The author has four

15

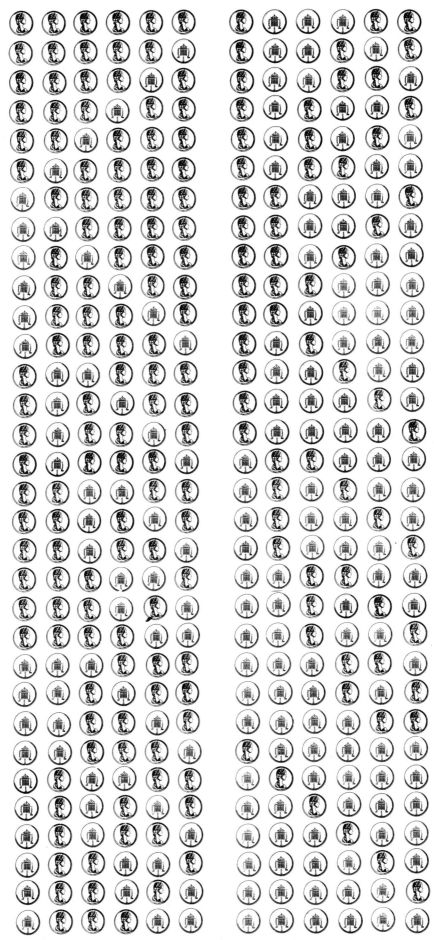

Diagram 2:1  The 64 possible results of six spins of a coin

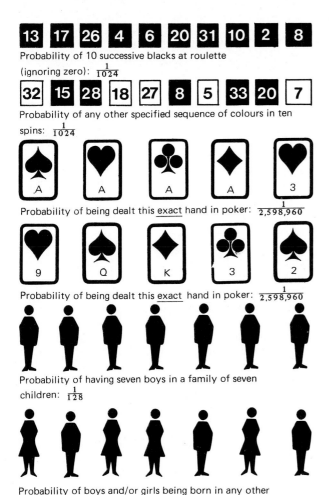

Probability of 10 successive blacks at roulette (ignoring zero): $\frac{1}{1024}$

Probability of any other specified sequence of colours in ten spins: $\frac{1}{1024}$

Probability of being dealt this <u>exact</u> hand in poker: $\frac{1}{2,598,960}$

Probability of being dealt this <u>exact</u> hand in poker: $\frac{1}{2,598,960}$

Probability of having seven boys in a family of seven children: $\frac{1}{128}$

Probability of boys and/or girls being born in any other specified order: $\frac{1}{128}$

Diagram 2:2 Novice gamblers would be wrong in thinking that the first sequence in each pair is less likely than the second. It is merely more easily distinguishable when it occurs

children, all of whom are girls, and has thus pulled off a 15–1 shot. It can easily be shown that no matter how many children one has (apart from two), the odds are always against an even distribution of the sexes. In order to get an even distribution, it is clear that before the final birth, one must have either one extra boy or one extra girl. Even if one has achieved this situation, it is still no better than an even chance that the last child will be of the correct sex to balance the numbers.

In a series of coups, where the alternative results are theoretically even, such as heads/tails, boys/girls, red/black in roulette (discounting the zero), it is called an equipartion when the incidence of the two alternatives is the same. One widely believed fallacy of the 'law of averages' is that the longer the series of coups, the more likely is equipartion, and indeed that in an infinite series equipartion is certain. In fact, the reverse is true. The odds are always against equipartion, and the longer the series continues, so the odds against get longer too. In a series of ten spins of a coin, the odds against equipartion are over 3–1 against; with 20 spins the odds are nearly 5–1 against.

The most expensive belief in the 'law of averages' is that which suggests that because in the long run chances will 'even out', a run of heads, say, will be followed by a run of tails. This is false. A coin has no knowledge of probabilities and is unaware that because it has landed twenty times consecutively head uppermost, a tail really is due. The probability of a head with a fair coin will always be $\frac{1}{2}$, irrespective of what has gone before. The contrary is a favourite belief of roulette players, who stake millions of chips each year on a colour because it has not won for three or four spins of the wheel. It is a belief which dies hard. An astonishing number of books on gambling will point out how false it is, and yet go on to expound systems with words like '...if staking on red, begin after a series of four consecutive blacks'. Such advice is not worth the paper it is advocated upon.

Imagine we are in a casino, playing roulette. Black has won ten times running (very unusual, but it happens). Four gamblers react in different ways. We will examine their reactions and evaluate them by awarding marks out of ten.

### Reaction No 1
Our first player says: 'Red is overdue. The law of averages says that these blacks will be cancelled out by a run of reds. I will stake heavily on red and await the profits.' He may wait a long time, as red is still no more likely than black. He is a candidate for mug punter of the year, and is so wrong that we must give him 0 out of 10.

### Reaction No 2
Our second player is better versed in the theory of probability. He says: 'A run of black must come sometime. Nothing remarkable here. I will continue with my system.' This is better. But suppose the run on black is due to an unsuspected bias or fault in the wheel? He can have 3 out of 10.

### Reaction No 3
Our third punter is a pragmatist. He says: 'Hello, there's something fishy here. The wheel is rigged, or the croupier is cheating. I will back black until I'm proved wrong.' There is something to be said for this view, since even if our gambler's suspicions are ill-founded, black is still as good a bet as red. But if the croupier *is* cheating, might he not continue to do so, and engineer some red winners to take our third player's money? Nevertheless 7 out of 10.

### Reaction No 4
Our fourth gambler is cautious. He says: 'Ten consecutive blacks is unusual. It is probably a legitimate sequence but I feel uneasy. I will not bet for a while; I will observe.' Splendid. 10 out of 10. One cannot fault a man who doesn't bet, unless one finds a cautious nature unattractive.

What then is this much quoted and seemingly fallacious law of averages? Is it a figment of the imaginations of a long line of optimistic gamblers?

No; it exists, although mathematicians prefer to call it the law of large numbers.

It states that:
If, in an event, the probability of a given outcome is $p$, and the event is repeated $n$ times, then the larger $n$ becomes, so the likelihood increases that the closer, in proportion, will be the occurrence of the given outcome to $np$.

To make this clearer, let us take an example. The event will be throwing a die, and the given outcome the throwing of a 6. When a die is thrown, there are six possible results, each with an equal chance of occurring. The probability, therefore, of throwing a 6 is $\frac{1}{6}$, or one chance in six.

The law of large numbers then tells us this:
In throwing a die, the probability of throwing a 6 is $\frac{1}{6}$. The more times the die is thrown, so the likelihood increases that the closer, in proportion, will be the number of 6s to $\frac{1}{6}$ of the number of throws.

It is in the disregard of the words 'in proportion' that most misconceptions arise. In 600 throws of a die, we might expect a 6 to occur about 100 times. We would not be unduly surprised if the deviation from our expectancy were 20 per cent, but we would if the number of 6s were 80 above or below the expected 100. In 600,000 throws, we would expect about 100,000 6s. Conversely we would not be surprised if the deviation were 80, but would be astonished were the deviation 20 per cent. The larger the number, the smaller will be the likely deviation, in percentage terms, but it will be larger in actual numbers.

In the law of large numbers, what is a large number? Paradoxically, whatever it is, it is never large enough. If the richest man in the world converted his fortune into pennies, and spun them all, would there be enough for him to be confident that he would get close to 50 per cent heads/50 per cent tails? Yes, but he would probably be even closer if 100 other men with similar fortunes joined him in the experiment, although the actual number of 'odd' heads or tails left over probably would be greater. If the two richest men in the world tossed a coin repeatedly and paid each other in pennies for a correct call, it is certain that one (could he live long enough) would eventually finish broke.

How can the law of large numbers be applied to gambling? Many systems rely on the theory that if one is backing red, say, in roulette and one gets behind because of an adverse run on black, the law of large numbers will ensure that red will eventually catch up. The probability of this can be assessed for any number of coups.

In Diagram 2:1, of the six spins of a coin, if one were backing heads, one would have lost the first spin on 32 occasions, and on 10 of these, heads would not have achieved equality at any stage of the six spins. So if backing heads, the probability of always being in arrears over a series of six spins is $\frac{10}{64}$. This is half the probability of an equipartion after six spins, which has already been shown to be $\frac{20}{64}$, and this ratio holds true for any number of spins. After 20 spins, the probability of equipartion is approximately $\frac{3}{17}$, and of being continuously in

Astronomer and mathematician Galileo

Pascal, who worked out probabilities concerning dice

## WAYS OF ACHIEVING A TOTAL OF NINE WITH THREE DICE (25)

## WAYS OF ACHIEVING A TOTAL OF TEN WITH THREE DICE (27)

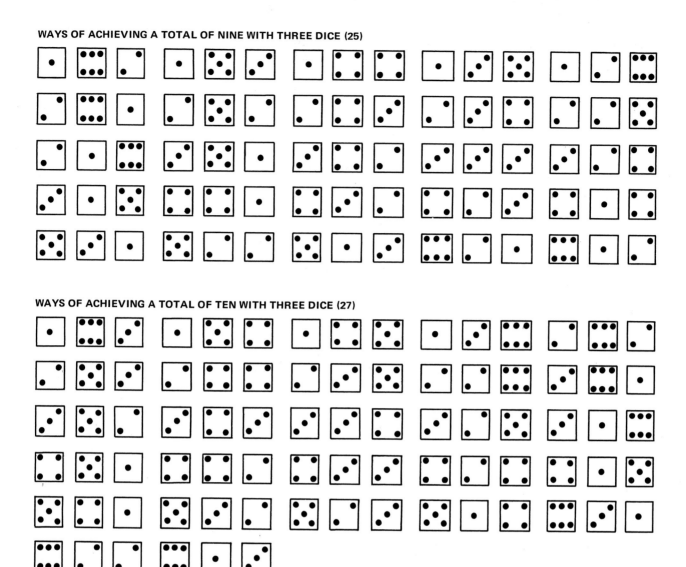

Diagram 2:3 The ways 9 and 10 can be thrown with three dice

arrears $\frac{3}{34}$. Therefore, if a system depends on an equipartion or better at any stage in 20 spins, it will lose once in about 12 trials.

Early observations on the theory of probability were made in the seventeenth century and concerned dice. The astronomer Galileo was asked by a gambling friend why, when three dice are thrown, the score of 10 appears more often than 9. Galileo demonstrated that as each die can fall in six ways, three dice can fall in a total of $6 \times 6 \times 6 = 216$ different ways. The number of spots uppermost can vary from 3 (three 1s) to 18 (three 6s). Some totals are more likely than others. For instance, 3 can only be achieved in one of the 216 ways (1,1,1), but 4 can be achieved three ways (1,1,2 – 1,2,1 – 2,1,1). Galileo pointed out that 10 can be achieved 27 ways, whereas 9 can be achieved only 25 ways. These ways are shown in Diagram 2:3. The probability of a total of 9 therefore is $\frac{25}{216}$; of 10 it is $\frac{27}{216}$. It says something for the astuteness of gamblers that this difference, of less than 1 per cent, was recognized before Galileo explained the mathematics of it.

Best known pioneer work on the theory of probability as applied to gambling was done by the French mathematician, Pascal. He was asked to solve a problem by the Chevalier de Méré. De Méré had won money by betting fellow-gamblers that he could throw a 6 in four throws of a die. He had then become more ambitious and had bet that with two dice he could throw a double-6 in 24 throws. Note that four is to six (the number of ways a single die can come to rest) as 24 is to 36 (the possible results from a pair of dice). However, the chevalier was slowly losing his money, and he asked Pascal why.

Now, if a 6 will occur on average once in six throws, the question is where in the course of six throws is the 'break-even' point, i.e. how many throws will it take before it is an even chance that a 6 will appear. The 6 might come on the first throw, or the sixth, or of course it need not appear at all in six throws. First thoughts might suggest that it is evens that it will appear in three throws, i.e. that if we divide a long series up into groups of six, the expected single 6 in each group will appear as often in the first three throws as the last three. However this ignores the probability that a 6, or any other number, will frequently appear twice in any group.

Pascal found the answer. If $n$ is the number we wish to find (in this case the number of throws necessary to make the throwing of a 6 an even proposition) and $\frac{1}{a}$ is the probability of succeeding at the first attempt (in this case $\frac{1}{6}$), then the formula is:

$$n = \frac{\log 2}{\log a - \log (a - 1)}$$

By substituting 6 for $a$, the answer to the problem is:

$$n = \frac{\log 2}{\log 6 - \log 5} = 3.8 \text{ approx.}$$

The break-even point for throwing a double-6 becomes:

$$n = \frac{\log 2}{\log 36 - \log 35} = 24.6 \text{ approx.}$$

Without log tables, a more approximate result can be obtained by multiplying the *odds to one* against achieving the desired result in one attempt by 0.693, which is the co-log of the hyperbolic log of 2.

The answers achieved by this method will be $5 \times 0.693 = 3.5$ approx. and $35 \times 0.693 = 24.3$ approx.

Therefore, by betting that he would throw a 6 in four throws of a single die, the Chevalier de Méré enjoyed odds in his favour (of about 5 per cent). However, he should have bet that he could throw a double-6 in 25 throws; by choosing 24 he was getting the worst of it (by about $2\frac{1}{2}$ per cent). By not allowing himself just one extra throw he was losing his money. The edge enjoyed by either party to a wager need not be very large for it to have a significant effect. It is also noteworthy that the chevalier, like many gamblers, could not understand the science which had proved his intuition wrong, and declared mathematics to be a swindle.

A calculation much used by gamblers is that concerned with the number of combinations of articles from a given larger number. For instance backers of horses want to know how many mixed doubles arise from a selection of, say, five horses; football-pool punters might need to know how many combinations of four draws arise from eight selections. Here again Pascal provides some guidance, in the system of numbers known as Pascal's Triangle. The first eight lines are shown in Diagram 2:4.

The triangle is easily formed: starting with a first line of two ones, each succeeding line is built up by adding together each pair of adjacent numbers in the line above.

We can grasp the significance of Pascal's Triangle by seeing how neatly line six summarizes the possible results of six spins of a coin set out in Diagram 2:1. Line six reads: 1,6,15,20,15,6,1, total 64. The coin-tossing diagram tells us that in six spins there is 1 way of achieving no heads, 6 ways of achieving one head, 15 ways of achieving two heads, 20 ways of achieving three heads, 15 ways of achieving four heads, 6 ways of achieving five heads, and 1 way of achieving six heads – a total of 64 possible results.

The question 'How many ways can two heads be thrown with six coins' is the same question as 'How many combinations of two can be obtained from six.' So Pascal's triangle can answer the two questions about combinations posed above. On line 5, the third term is 10 (remember that the first term represents o heads, the second 1 and the *third* 2). So there are ten combinations of two from five. Notice there are also ten combinations of three (for every group of two from five, there must be a group of three remaining). The number of combinations of four draws from eight matches is found from the fifth term in line eight, i.e. 70.

However, there is no need to draw diagrams like Diagram 2:1 or Pascal's Triangle in order to work out combinations. There is a simple formula. The shorthand for writing the number of combinations available from a given total is $^nC_a$, where $n$ is the total number and $a$ the number of articles required in each group. For instance, eight articles taken four at a time is written $^8C_4$, and we've seen that the answer is 70. This can be calculated by a simple fraction. The denominator is 4 (the number in the combination) $\times 3 \times 2 \times 1$. The numerator is the same number of terms, beginning with the total number of articles and diminishing by 1, in this case $8 \times 7 \times 6 \times 5$.

So the fraction is:

$$\frac{8 \times 7 \times 6 \times 5}{4 \times 3 \times 2 \times 1} = 70$$

It is possible by the same formula to calculate the number of bridge or whist hands from a full pack of cards, $^{52}C_{13}$.

The fraction is:

$$\frac{52 \times 51 \times 50 \times 49 \times 48 \times 47 \times 46 \times 45 \times 44 \times 43 \times 42 \times 41 \times 40}{13 \times 12 \times 11 \times 10 \times 9 \times 8 \times 7 \times 6 \times 5 \times 4 \times 3 \times 2 \times 1}$$

This, of course, is a mammoth calculation, but an approximate answer can be quickly obtained with logarithm tables. With a table of logs of factorials it can be done in a minute or so. The fraction's denominator (13 multiplied by all the numbers smaller than itself) is known as factorial 13, usually written 13! If one multiplies the numerator

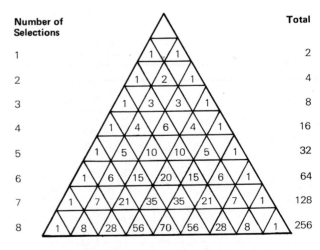

| Number of Selections | | Total |
|---|---|---|
| 1 | 1  1 | 2 |
| 2 | 1  2  1 | 4 |
| 3 | 1  3  3  1 | 8 |
| 4 | 1  4  6  4  1 | 16 |
| 5 | 1  5  10  10  5  1 | 32 |
| 6 | 1  6  15  20  15  6  1 | 64 |
| 7 | 1  7  21  35  35  21  7  1 | 128 |
| 8 | 1  8  28  56  70  56  28  8  1 | 256 |

Diagram 2:4 The first eight lines of Pascal's Triangle

Diagram 2:5 The six orders in which three horses can finish a race

by 39! it will be seen that it becomes 52! So if we multiply both numerator and denominator by 39!, the fraction becomes:

$$\frac{52!}{13! \times 39!}$$

To work this out involves looking up the log of 13!, adding it to log 39!, deducting the sum from log 52! and looking up the answer in anti-log tables. How near the answer will be to the correct figure of 635,013,559,600 depends on whether one uses tables of 4,5,7 or more figures. The number of possible five-card poker hands or ten-card gin rummy hands can be calculated in the same way.

The difference between a combination and a permutation is this: a combination is the number of ways $a$ articles can be taken from a total of $n$ articles, for example any three draws from a selection of eight. A permutation is the number of ways $a$ articles can be taken from $n$ articles, *in a specified order*. Football-pool fans will realize that what are called pools permutations are not permutations at all, but combinations.

If we aim to select the first three in a horse race in the *correct order*, and wish to cover five horses in our bet, we have five alternative horses to finish first. For each of these five, any one of the remaining four could finish second, and for each permutation of first and second there are three horses left to fill the third place. So the total number of ways of forecasting first, second and third from five horses is $5 \times 4 \times 3 = 60$. This is a permutation. If we are required to name the first three *in any order*, then we can cover every eventuality from our five selections with 10 bets, any three from five being:

$$\frac{5 \times 4 \times 3}{3 \times 2 \times 1} = 10$$

This is a combination. It will be noticed that it requires 6 times more bets to name the horses in the correct order. This can be verified. The three horses in each of the 10 combinations can finish in any one of six different ways (see Diagram 2:5). So to place any three from five in the correct order requires $10 \times 6 = 60$ bets.

A favourite bet among racing men, particularly in British betting shops, is the Yankee, which involves backing four horses (in separate races) in six doubles, four trebles and a four-horse accumulator – 11 bets in all. Whenever a punter is successful with his first three selections, feverish calculations go on to discover how much has already been won and how much is going on to the fourth horse. There is a short cut to solving these questions.

First of all it must be known how to calculate the return from a simple double. Suppose the winning horses were returned at 4–1 and 7–1. Add one point to the odds of each horse, and multiply them: $5 \times 8 = 40$, which is the number of units the punter collects (less tax). Sometimes fractions are involved but the principle remains the same. A point added to each of 7–2 and 9–4 gives 9–2 and 13–4 (9–4 being $2\frac{1}{4}$–1, a point added, $3\frac{1}{4}$–1, gives 13–4. It is necessary only to add the 4 to the 9 to get the figure 13). Multiplying $\frac{13}{4}$ by $\frac{9}{2}$ gives $\frac{117}{8}$ or $14\frac{5}{8}$ points, which the punter collects. Winnings from trebles and accumulators are calculated in the same way.

If four horses, A,B,C and D are backed in a £1 Yankee (£11 staked) and A,B and C have won, the bets to have won so far are the doubles AB,AC and BC and the treble ABC. Returns so far then are AB + AC + BC + ABC. This can be simplified to AB(1 + C) + C(A + B). A's price was 2–1, B was 4–1 and C was 7–2. Add a point to these odds and substitute them in the formula. This gives:

$$(3 \times 5)(1 + \tfrac{9}{2}) + \tfrac{9}{2}(3 + 5) = 118 \cdot 5$$

Therefore the punter already has £118.50 to come even if D loses. To calculate his bet on D he must add this amount to the odds of A, B and C (adding one point to each, as before). Thus:

$$118 \cdot 5 + 3 + 5 + \tfrac{9}{2} = 131$$

The punter has, therefore, £118.50 'in the bank' plus £131 going on to horse D.

It will be seen from these calculations that the amount of money being bet on the fourth horse of a Yankee is always more than the amount won on the first three winners. It is not a bet for the faint-hearted!

A knowledge of probabilities is necessary to enable a gambler to work out whether a proposed bet is equitable or 'fair'. If the bet is being struck in a betting shop, on a racecourse, or in a casino, it is practically certain that it will not be equitable, so the exercise becomes one of calculating the percentage against the punter.

If a punter backs black on a roulette wheel, he has 18 chances of winning, and if there is one zero on the wheel, he will have 19 chances of losing (let us assume, for ease of reckoning, that all stakes are lost on zero – not necessarily the case, as the chapter on roulette will show). On 37 spins, then, the punter can 'expect' to win 18 times, and since the bank pays even money for black, he will receive 36 chips (one staked and one won for each black). He will have staked 37 chips and his 'expectancy' is 36 chips. From the casino's point of view, it will win 1 chip for every 37 staked, or 2·7 per cent approx. Where even-money bets are put in prison (see Chapter

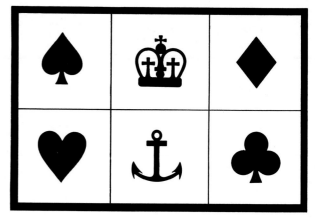

Diagram 2:6 Crown and Anchor board

| | | | Possible Ways | Probability |
|---|---|---|---|---|
| ⚓ | ⚓ | ⚓ | 1 x 1 x 1 = 1 | $\frac{1}{216}$ |
| ⚓ | ⚓ | | 1 x 1 x 5 = 5 | $\frac{5}{216}$ |
| ⚓ | | ⚓ | 1 x 5 x 1 = 5 | $\frac{5}{216}$ |
| | ⚓ | ⚓ | 5 x 1 x 1 = 5 | $\frac{5}{216}$ |
| ⚓ | | | 1 x 5 x 5 = 25 | $\frac{25}{216}$ |
| | ⚓ | | 5 x 1 x 5 = 25 | $\frac{25}{216}$ |
| | | ⚓ | 5 x 5 x 1 = 25 | $\frac{25}{216}$ |
| | | | 5 x 5 x 5 = 125 | $\frac{125}{216}$ |

Diagram 2:7 The possible results in respect of the Anchor

Five) when zero appears, the casino's percentage is 1·4 approx. This is small, but remember the Chevalier de Méré and his extra throw: it is quite enough for the casino proprietor.

A percentage of 2·7 against the gambler does not mean that he can take £100 into a casino and 'expect' to emerge with £97.30. With a bank of £100 he might have 300 bets at £5 each with his money before the night is out. Although the same money is being staked over and over again, his effective stakes are £1500 and he should not be surprised if he loses something like $15 \times £2.7$ and is left with only about £59.50.

As a more complicated example of working out the percentage against the gambler, let us consider the game of Crown and Anchor. The board is shown in Diagram 2:6. Stakes are placed on any of the six alternatives. Three dice (whose six sides show the four suits, the Crown and the Anchor) are then thrown to determine the winners. Imagine a gullible sailor decides to stake £1 on the Anchor. The banker or operator will pay him evens for one Anchor uppermost on the dice (£2 back), 2–1 for two

Anchors (£3 back) and 3–1 for three (£4 back). The sailor reckons that at least one Anchor is an even-money proposition from three dice ($\frac{1}{6} + \frac{1}{6} + \frac{1}{6} = \frac{1}{2}$), that the extra payout for two or three Anchors is a bonus, and that he is on to a good thing.

Is he? First of all, his mathematics are at fault as he has *added* the probabilities in three separate events. One can only add probabilities if they are mutually exclusive. For instance, the probability of throwing any one of an Anchor, a Crown or a Heart with one die *is* $\frac{1}{6} + \frac{1}{6} + \frac{1}{6} = \frac{1}{2}$, since any one of these results automatically rules out the other two. Had the sailor applied his theory to assessing the probability of tossing at least one head with three coins, he might have estimated it at $\frac{1}{2} + \frac{1}{2} + \frac{1}{2} = 1\frac{1}{2}$. Since the probabilities range from 0 (an impossibility) to 1 (a certainty), a probability of $1\frac{1}{2}$ is clearly a nonsense.

In fact, the three dice can fall in any one of 216 ways ($6 \times 6 \times 6$). These are summarized in respect of the Anchor, in Diagram 2:7.

So the sailor, if he bet 216 times and all the possible results appeared once, would have:

1 bet where three Anchors occurred and be paid back £4;
15 bets where two Anchors occurred and be paid back $15 \times £3 = £45$;
75 bets where one Anchor occurred and be paid back $75 \times £2 = £150$;
125 bets where no Anchor occurred and be paid back nothing.

So he would stake £216, be paid back £199 and lose therefore £17.

The banker expects to win nearly £8 of every £100 staked. In other words he has a percentage of nearly 8 per cent in his favour, a considerable advantage.

The calculations of the specific percentages against the gambler for various bets at roulette, craps, horse racing and others, together with an examination of popular systems, will be found in the appropriate chapters.

An awareness of the theory of probability can be fun. It enables one to understand better one's insurance policies (actuaries are experts on probability) and the fluctuations of the stock market and interest rates. It allows one to spot ambiguities and evasions in advertisements, company reports and the statistics of politicians. It provides wry amusement. In the film *Twelve Angry Men*, a lone juror is advocating a not-guilty verdict. After a persuasive argument he forces a secret ballot among the eleven holding out for a guilty verdict. It is clear that one of them will change his mind. As the slips are unfolded and read, and the beads of perspiration appear, it is also clear that for the greatest dramatic effect the 'Not Guilty' slip should be the last. But it is 10–1 against this. Will director Sydney Lumet have the nerve to sustain the suspense in the face of such odds? No, he makes the vital slip the second last. Perhaps he thinks odds of 9–2 against it being one of the last two are both mathematically and dramatically acceptable.

Finally, a personal reminiscence. In a game of Monopoly, the author once built hotels on his first throw. This can be achieved in only one way. It involves throwing a double-1 with the dice, landing on Community Chest, drawing the card which says 'Go Back to Old Kent Road', buying it, throwing another double-1 to land on Whitechapel Road, buying that and building hotels before taking the third throw allowed by the throwing of two doubles. As there are 16 cards in the Community Chest pile, the probability of achieving such a feat is

$$\frac{1}{36 \times 16 \times 36},$$

or odds of 20,735 to 1. He has forgotten who won the game, and a few hundred other less spectacular throws, but will always remember the pleasure of pulling off such a long shot.

Examining the slips in *Twelve Angry Men*

## Chapter 3

# Private CARD GAMES

The origin of the standard pack of playing cards is uncertain. It no doubt developed from several sources: perhaps early paper currency, or fortune-telling devices like bones or sticks. The variety of games a pack of cards allows is limitless. New games are being devised all the time and few such simple inventions can have provided so many people all over the world with so much enjoyment for so long a period.

Cards were used for fortune-telling before the first card games were played. The Tarot pack, the forerunner of the now universal pack, is still widely used for fortune-telling purposes. It is a splendid pictorial pack. The earliest Tarot packs of the fourteenth century had four suits: Cups, which became Hearts; Swords, which became Spades; Money, or Gold Pieces, which became Diamonds; and Batons or Clubs, which remained Clubs. Each suit had ten numbered cards, as does the present pack, and four pictures: the King, Queen, Knight and Knave. There were also 22 trumps, numbered 0–21 and representing figures, bodies of the universe or ideas, such as the Fool, the Emperor, the Pope, the Star, the Moon, the World, Death, Temperance or Justice. There were thus 78 cards in the Tarot pack, and the modern pack was formed when the 22 trumps and the four Knights were dropped. The stylised suit symbols are now general, although the names given to them are not. Hearts are still Cups in Spain, while Spades are Pikes in Italy, Germany and France and Swords in Spain.

Most card games can be played for stakes, from the highly complex bridge, which requires considerable skill to play well, to the children's game of Sevens or Fan Tan. However, a few games are recognized and played as pure gambling games, and these are described here. In private card games, of course, there is no percentage lost to a casino or bank, and all players have equal chances of winning or losing.

## Poker

Poker is the most widely played private gambling game. There are many variations, but the main objects of the game remain the same. The most popular form, straight-draw poker, is described first. The 52-card pack is used, the cards ranking from Ace high down to 2, although in 'straights' the Ace can count low. Any reasonable number may play, and the deal passes in rotation clockwise round the table. Players form a 'pot' by each contributing an agreed amount. Five cards are then dealt to each player, and, beginning with the player on the dealer's left, each may either bet or drop. A player who drops discards his hand and takes no further

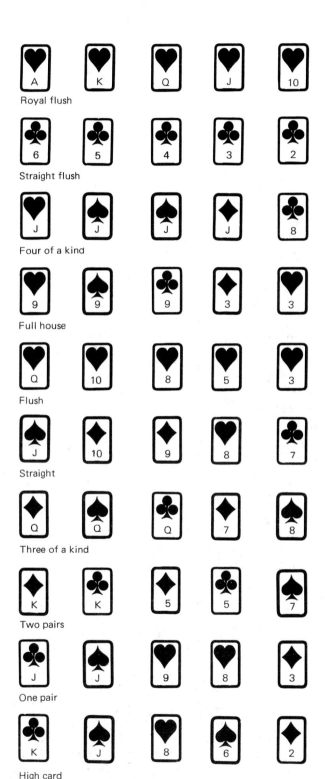

Diagram 3:1 The rank of the classes of poker hand: highest at the top

Jack of Clubs
French

Queen of Hearts
French

King of Diamonds
French

King of Diamonds
English

Nineteenth century playing cards: French Jack of Clubs, Queen of Hearts, King of Diamonds and English King of Diamonds Modern cards: Jack of Clubs, Queen of Hearts, King of Diamonds and Queen of Spades

part in that deal. Each player contrives to get the best poker hand; later it will be seen how he may improve his hand by discarding cards and drawing others. The rank of the various hands is shown in Diagram 3:1.

It is advisable before the game to agree on a minimum and maximum stake. If the first player decides to stay in the game, he may place any stake he wishes in the pot—let us say it is one unit. In practice, players usually place their stakes in front of them, so that at all times the other players can check that the stakes are correct. To stay in the game, a succeeding player must place at least one unit into the pot. A player who puts one unit into the pot is said to call. Alternatively, he may raise. Let us say he puts three units into the pot, which means he raises by two. The betting will then continue round the table till it reaches him again, by which time all players remaining in the game will have placed three units into the pot, unless in the meantime another player or players have raised again, when the betting continues still further. The first betting interval ends when all players have placed the same amount in the pot. At each turn a player may drop out, call or raise, but if a player drops, the stakes he has already contributed to the pot remain in and are lost.

After the first betting interval, the players may exchange any number of their cards by discarding them and receiving fresh ones from the dealer. There is then another betting interval which follows the pattern of the first. Players disappointed by their draw will probably drop immediately. It is possible all may drop except one, who will then take the pot without the need to show his cards. Otherwise, as soon as all bets are again equal, there is a showdown, and the highest hand takes the pot. If two hands are of the same rank, the higher combination wins; for example three Aces beat three Kings, and two pairs, of Jacks and Threes, beat two pairs of Tens and Nines. If the combinations are of the same value, the highest odd card wins; for example a pair of Jacks with Ace the highest odd card beats a pair of Jacks and a Queen.

**Pot-deals** in poker are very popular. If a *Jack-pot* is being played, a player may not open the betting unless he has a pair of Jacks or better, although players without do not have to drop. A player who opens will have to show his cards when he drops to prove his hand was eligible to open. In a progressive

Steve McQueen and Edward G. Robinson play stud poker in *The Cincinatti Kid*

Jack-pot, if no player bets, the next deal is a Queen-pot and so on.

**Stud poker** is an interesting variation of the game. Players are dealt a card face down, known as their 'hole card', and then a second face up. The player with the highest card showing opens the betting. If two cards are equal, the player nearer the dealer's left opens. Betting continues until all bets are equalized, as in draw poker. A second face-up card is then dealt, and there is another betting interval, the player with the highest combination of the two cards opening the betting. Straights and flushes are not recognized in this context, and a player holding 10 6 opens in preference to a player with 4 5 of Hearts. The alternate dealing of a face-up card and betting continues until all players have been dealt five cards, including their hole card. Players may drop at any time. The dealer is expected to point out which player is required to open at each betting interval, and also when he is dealing the third and fourth face-up cards to indicate possible straights or flushes. Thus when dealing a Heart to a player with only Hearts showing he should announce 'possible flush'. When the players left in the game each have five cards the final betting interval takes place, and when bets are equalized the players turn over their hole cards for the showdown.

**Poker variations.** There are many different poker games and each game can be played with different rules. In *High-Low Poker*, for instance, the pot is divided between the holders of the highest and lowest hands at the showdown. In some poker games the player on the dealer's left is required to put an agreed stake, known as an 'ante', in the pot, the next player puts in a 'straddle', twice the amount of the ante, and the third player opens the betting. In all poker games an additional option to dropping out, calling or raising can be allowed by agreement. It is known as checking. The player whose turn it is to stake first in each betting interval (the player on the dealer's left, or the player with the highest combination showing in stud poker) may check, and remain in the game without increasing his stake. Subsequent players may do the same, until a player raises, when, of course, all other players are required to equal his stake. In all poker games wild cards may be used by prior agreement. The Joker may be added to the pack as a solitary wild card, or black Twos, or all four Twos, may be wild. At the showdown, players are required to state which cards their wild cards represent. With wild cards, a new rank of hand is possible: five of a kind. It is the highest hand.

**Poker strategy.** It is claimed by good poker players that poker is a more skilful game than bridge. This assertion is based on the belief that a good poker player can win more consistently and surely than a good bridge player. The good player is required to have some idea of the mathematical odds against improving any hand he is dealt by the draw, and as there are 2,598,960 possible poker hands in a 52-card pack, this is a tall order. He must consider the size of the pot and calculate how much he might expect to win in relation to the stake required to remain in the game. He must know the practice of the other players and be able to judge if they are bluffing or not. He must be able to estimate the strength of his opponents' hands by the number of cards they draw and the way they bet. At the same time he must vary his own betting strategy to deny the other players the same information about himself. Above all, he must cultivate a 'poker face'. Such skills can only come from the study of books dealing exclusively with the game and from long practice as a player. Beginners should accept that they are likely to lose to regular players, and should limit their bets accordingly.

# Brag

Brag is a sort of mini-poker popular in Britain. The original game is thought to be the ancestor of poker. Only three cards are dealt to each player and there is one betting interval. There is no draw. In the traditional game there are only three classes of hand, pair-royal (three of a kind), pair and highest card, but 'braggers' or wild cards are used and a hand with a bragger is inferior to one of an equal rank without. In the more popular modern version, straights, more often called 'runs', and flushes are recognized, and wild cards are not normally used. The rank of the classes of hand is shown in Diagram 3:2.

It will be noticed that a run beats a flush. With a three-card hand, as opposed to a five-card poker hand, a run is less common than a flush. Three of a kind is called a 'prial'. With hands of equal rank, the higher combination wins, except that a prial of Threes is the highest hand, and beats a prial of Aces. Ace is optionally high or low in sequences, and A 2 3 usually beats A K Q. To avoid arguments this should be agreed before play begins. The deal passes to the left, the dealer usually places an agreed amount in the 'kitty', as the pool or pot is known, and players in turn to his left have the choice of dropping, calling or raising. When bets are equalized, there is a showdown, the best hand taking the kitty.

# Rummy

Rummy is a very popular game and may be played by two to six people. The standard pack is used, the cards ranking from King high down to Ace. With 2–4 players, the dealer deals seven cards to each player including himself; with 5 or 6 players he

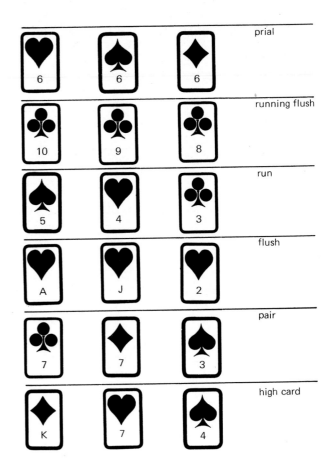

Diagram 3:2 The rank of the classes of brag hand: highest at the top

deals six. He then places the next card face up in the centre of the table to begin a discard pile, and the remainder are placed face down to form the stock. Each player in turn to the dealer's left may take either the top card of the discard pile into his hand or the top card of the stock, discarding a card himself. The object of the game is to form sets, either of three or four cards of the same value, for example three or four Jacks, or a sequence of at least three cards of the same suit, say 4 5 6 of Hearts. As the Ace counts low, A 2 3 is a sequence, A K Q is not. Players may also 'lay off' odd cards on other players' sets. Sets may be declared or cards laid off only on the player's turn. When a player has got rid of all his cards he wins and the deal ends. A player going out need not make a discard. Other players may lay off cards onto the winner's sets, and are caught for the values of all cards remaining in their hands, including undeclared sets. Court cards count as ten, other cards at their pip values. Settlement is made to the winner after each deal at an amount per pip to be agreed beforehand. A player who declares all his cards in one turn scores rummy and is paid double.

**Knock rummy** is a variation in which sets are not declared. The deal ends when a player 'knocks', which he may do whenever it is his turn by laying down his hand. It may contain unmatched cards (i.e. cards not in sets), which count against him. As in the parent game, court cards count as ten, other cards as their pip values. The other players then lay

Omar Sharif, film star and world-class bridge player, whose matches are sometimes for £1 a point

down their hands, and the player with the lowest total in unmatched cards wins. Cards are not laid off and settlement is made as in the parent game. If the knocker does not win, he pays an additional ten points to the winner. If another player's count equals that of the knocker, he wins, but does not collect from the knocker. If two other players tie, they share the winnings. A player who knocks with a rummy (all cards in sets) collects a bonus of 25 points from each player. If another player has a rummy, he loses and must pay the knocker the 25-point bonus.

**Gin rummy** is an American version of knock rummy for two players. Ten cards are dealt to each player. If the non-dealer refuses the upcard, the dealer may have it. If he refuses, the non-dealer draws the top card of the stock. After drawing once, either player may knock on his own turn, provided his total in unmatched cards does not exceed ten. His opponent then lays down his hand and may lay off unmatched cards on the knocker's sets. If the knocker has the lower count he scores the difference in points. If his opponent has an equal or lower count, he scores the difference, if any, and a bonus of 25. If the knocker goes 'gin', i.e. all his cards are matched, he scores a bonus of 25, even if his opponent then matches all his cards. The first player to score 100 wins the game, and adds 100 points to his score as game bonus. Each player then adds to his score 25 points for each hand he has won. If the loser has no points, the winner's score is doubled.

Settlement is then made at an agreed amount per point, or per ten points.

**Rummy variations.** All rummy players have their own favourite version of the game and practice varies considerably, especially when knocking, laying off and settling. Players must agree before play begins on which conventions are to be followed.

## Whist

Whist has lost much of its popularity with the rise of bridge but for many years it was popular as a medium for mild gambling and as an excuse for a pleasant social evening because of the prevalence of whist drives. These were, and are, often organized for local good causes.

Four players take part as two pairs, partners sitting opposite each other. Each player cuts for deal; highest deals. In this context Ace counts low, but in the play Ace is high and the cards rank in usual order down to 2. All 52 cards are dealt, the dealer turning the last card, his own, face up to denote trumps. The player to the left of the dealer leads a card, and other players must follow suit if possible, otherwise they may trump or discard. The four cards played constitute a trick, and the highest card of the suit led, or the highest trump, wins the trick. One player collects all the tricks for his side. At the end of the hand, the deal passes clockwise round the table. Scoring and settlement are optional, but traditionally each side scores a point for each trick above six made in one hand, and the game is won by the first side to reach either 5 or 7 points.

In whist drives, each table consists of two partnerships formed by a lady and a gentleman (gentility is a feature of whist drives), and after each hand the winning gentleman moves up one table to form a partnership with the losing lady there, and the winning lady moves down a table to partner the losing gentleman there. Totals of tricks won are kept by each player on a score-card, and at the end of the drive there are usually prizes for the winning lady and the winning gentleman, plus a booby prize for the lowest score. Players entering whist drives for the first time should be warned that there are conventions accepted by regular players, for instance a player holding A K Q J of the trump suit is expected to inform his partner of the fact by leading Jack first followed by Queen. A player contravening these conventions might get a black look from his partner.

**Solo whist** is a more serious gambling medium. As its name implies, there are no partnerships, each player playing for himself. The deal passes in rotation, and the cards are not shuffled after each hand. The dealer deals the cards to the players in bundles of three, the last four cards being dealt singly. The last card is dealt face up to denote trumps. Beginning with the player to the dealer's left, each player assesses his hand and may pass or make a bid as follows.

*Solo* indicates that he undertakes to make five tricks.
*Misère* is an undertaking to lose all thirteen tricks. There are no trumps with this bid.
*Abundance* is an undertaking to win nine tricks, with a trump suit of his choice.

*Royal abundance* is an undertaking to win nine tricks, with the turned-up suit as trumps.

*Open misère* is an undertaking to lose all thirteen tricks, with, after the first trick, his hand exposed on the table. There are no trumps.

*Abundance declared* is an undertaking to win all thirteen tricks with a trump suit of his choice.

Any bid made must be higher than a previous bid, and a player who passes may not later enter the bidding. A player who fulfils his contract, or fails to, wins or loses to each opponent at the following rate: 2 units for solo, 3 for misère, 4 for abundance or royal abundance, 6 for open misère and 8 for abundance declared. There are no additional bonuses or penalties for over or under-tricks.

A further combined bid, known as *proposal and acceptance*, is sometimes allowed. A player proposing undertakes to win five tricks in partnership with another player, and a player accepting agrees to form the partnership. The contract is worth two points, received or paid to the other two players. It is generally considered an insignificant and time-wasting bid and is usually ignored by present-day players.

It should be realized that as the cards are not shuffled, and are dealt in bundles, hands are 'freak' hands. A player with, say, eight trumps should consider the possibility of four or five of the trumps against him being in the same hand. Good bidding comes from experience. It is soon learnt, for instance, that a player bidding misère on the strength of a long suit which lacks the 2 is often heading for trouble.

# Napoleon

Napoleon is a game similar to solo, suitable for 2–6 players. The deal passes in rotation, and five cards from the full pack are dealt to each player. Players bid to make two, three, four or five tricks. A bid of five is known as 'nap'. Only one round of bidding is allowed, and the highest bidder leads to the first trick, the first card led indicating the trump suit. The declarer wins or loses to each player at the following rate: for Two, 2 units; for Three, 3 units; for Four, 4 units. A player bidding nap wins 10 units from each player if successful, but loses only 5 units to each if he fails. Napoleon is a very simple game, attractive to gamblers who like fast action.

# Pontoon

Pontoon has the same roots as blackjack, which is popular in American casinos, and which is fully described in the following chapter. It is also known as *vingt-et-un*, and is played in one form or another all over the world. It was the most popular game of British soldiers during the First World War, and the version described here is that most found at private card sessions in Britain. Up to ten may play with the standard 52-card pack. First banker is decided by cutting, Ace being high, and the banker deals a card face down to each player including himself. Each player except the banker looks at his card and stakes accordingly. It is advisable to agree a minimum and maximum stake before playing.

The object of the game is to achieve as near as possible a total of 21, Ace counting as 1 or 11 at the discretion of its holder, court cards as 10 and other cards at their pip value.

When all players have staked, the banker deals a second card to all players, himself included. A player dealt two Aces may split them by putting up a stake equal to his original stake on the second Ace and regarding each Ace as the first card dealt to him, receiving a second card to each.

The banker then deals with each player in turn, beginning on his left. A player satisfied with his two-card total stands. Players may stand on totals between 16 and 21. Alternatively, he may buy additional cards, but cannot hold more than five. He may buy each card by increasing his stake by any amount not greater than his original stake. A player with a four-card total of eleven or less must announce that he cannot bust and his fifth card must be twisted. A third option open to the player at any time is to twist, which means he receives an additional free card face up. He may twist as often as he wishes, provided his hand does not exceed five cards. A player who once twists may not subsequently buy a card. If in buying a card, or twisting, a player's total count exceeds 21, he busts and loses immediately and the banker collects his stake.

The highest hand is a 'pontoon', formed by an Ace and a 10 or court card. A player holding this hand declares it immediately by turning his cards over. A five-card hand beats any other except a pontoon.

When all players have stood or bust, the banker turns over his cards. If he has a pontoon, he wins from all players. Otherwise he may stand or deal himself as many additional cards as he pleases. If he exceeds 21, he pays all players still in the game. If he achieves a five-card hand, he wins from all players except those with a pontoon. When he decides to stand, he wins from all players with an inferior or equal total to himself, and loses to those with a superior total and to those with five-card hands.

In some schools a player who holds three 7s wins triple his stake from the bank, unless the banker holds a pontoon.

A player holding a pontoon takes over the bank on the next deal, unless the pontoon is held on a split hand or unless the banker also holds a pontoon. If two or more players hold a pontoon, the player nearest the banker's left takes the bank. Otherwise the banker retains the bank.

The banker holds a considerable advantage in pontoon, due to his privilege in playing last. He can draw according to his estimate of the strength of the hands against him, and of course he wins from all players who bust even though he may bust himself. He also has the advantage of winning all tied hands.

There is room for skill in the game, and a player using sound principles will invariably win. A beginner, while awaiting his turn of the bank, might do worse than stake the maximum on Aces, always splitting a pair, half the maximum on 10s, and a minimum stake on all other cards, except perhaps 2s and 3s. He might venture a slightly higher stake on 2s and 3s and buy while he continues to draw

Cowpunchers relaxing with an open-air game of cards

small cards. If his two-card total is 10 or 11 he might buy, otherwise he might twist. He might always stand as soon as he has a legitimate total, although he might twist a fifth card if his four-card total is 16. A player following this system should not lose too much while not holding the bank, and he will be unlucky if he does not make a handsome profit from his spells with the bank.

## Hoggenheimer

Hoggenheimer is not a well-known game compared to those already described, but roulette players enjoy it because the placing of the stakes on the layout and the bets available are evocative of roulette. Indeed, the game is sometimes known as English roulette. It is played with the standard pack, minus the 6s, 5s, 4s, 3s and 2s and with the addition of the Joker. If the Joker is recognizable because of its comparative cleanliness, one of the discarded 2s can take its place. The bank is held by each player in turn for five coups. The cards are dealt face down in four rows of eight, the odd card being placed face down to one side. When the players have placed their bets, the odd card is turned face up and put in its place in the layout. The top row in the layout is reserved for Spades, Ace down to 7, the second row for Hearts, the third for Diamonds, the fourth for Clubs. The card replaced in the layout is turned over and put in its own appointed place and so on until the Joker is turned up, when the coup ends.

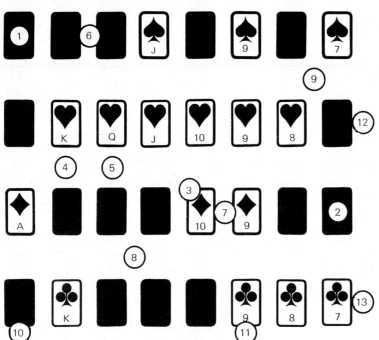

Diagram 3:3 A completed game of hoggenheimer. For explanation, see text.

Marked cards with the markings exaggerated. Top, Ace; centre, King; bottom, Queen

Bettors are paid by the banker if the card or group of cards they have backed are turned up at the end of the game. Diagram 3:3 shows a completed game, the Joker having just been turned up.

Stake 1 is bet on the Ace of Spades, Stake 2 on the 7 of Diamonds and Stake 3 on the 10 of Diamonds. Odds paid on these bets might be even money, and the gambler who has backed the 10 of Diamonds has won his bet; the others have lost.

Stake 4 is bet on the two red Kings and Stake 5 on the red Queens. Stake 6 is on the K Q of Spades and Stake 7 on the 10 9 of Diamonds. Odds are 2–1 and the last bet has won; the others lost.

Stake 8 is placed on the Q J of Diamonds and the Q J of Clubs, and Stake 9 on the 8 7 of Spades and the 8 7 of Hearts. Odds are 4–1 and both have lost, the former comprehensively.

Stake 10 is bet on the four Aces, Stake 11 on the four 9s. Odds are again 4–1. The first is lost, but the gambler who backed the four 9s has won.

Stake 12 has been placed on the Heart suit, and the gambler has nearly brought off a good win. Stake 13 is on the Club suit. Odds against a suit are 8–1.

The odds quoted should ensure a small profit for the banker. The game offers a variety of bets at differing odds.

## Cheating

Cheating at cards is far more common than the most cynical casual player would imagine, and the most accomplished cheats use methods as sophisticated as those of modern business. No skill and little practice are required to cheat with a marked pack, and thousands of marked packs are manufactured and sold every week. Ostensibly they are sold as con-

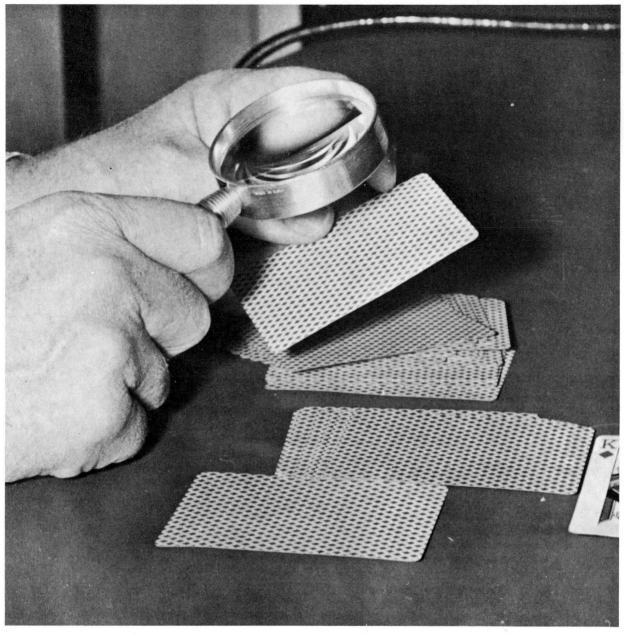

A Nevada Gaming Commission agent looking for markings in a Las Vegas casino

juror's props, but how many are used in poker schools by players whose only pretensions to magic are to make their opponents' wallets thinner? A man who knows all the hole-cards dealt in stud poker can win as much as he wants. Cards can be marked to be instantly identifiable to those who know the key, while others might not find the marks even if told they were there.

The 'mechanic' needs no mechanical aids. By false shuffles and cuts he can place a single card or even a sequence of cards just where he wants it in the pack. He can peek at cards in a dozen ways without arousing suspicion, deal off the bottom so quickly it is undetectable and palm cards for use at any time. Cheats frequently work in pairs or groups while carefully concealing their acquaintanceship. Where two cheats are playing, each deals the other the good hands. Or the accomplice need only watch: a scratch of an ear, touch of a tie or even a hand in a pocket can convey to a partner where the dangerous cards lie.

Cheats do not cheat all the time. Illegitimate knowledge of a card or two every few hands is enough to give them the advantage they need. Nor are they necessarily strangers. The friend known for months in the club might well have joined in order ultimately to get into the card school. Needless to say he does not have a Damon Runyon name or wear a battered snap-brimmed hat above an unshaven chin.

All card players must take on trust the integrity of those they play with. It is useless to be neurotic about cheating, but it is sensible to be aware of the possibilities, and to withdraw quickly if suspicions are aroused. It is a good policy not to play with strangers. This should be an invariable rule on trains travelling to race meetings. Far better to read a book and reserve one's capital for the horses. Their form will be less predictable than that of the gentleman idly shuffling a pack in one corner of the compartment or the gentleman in the other corner who innocently suggests a friendly game.

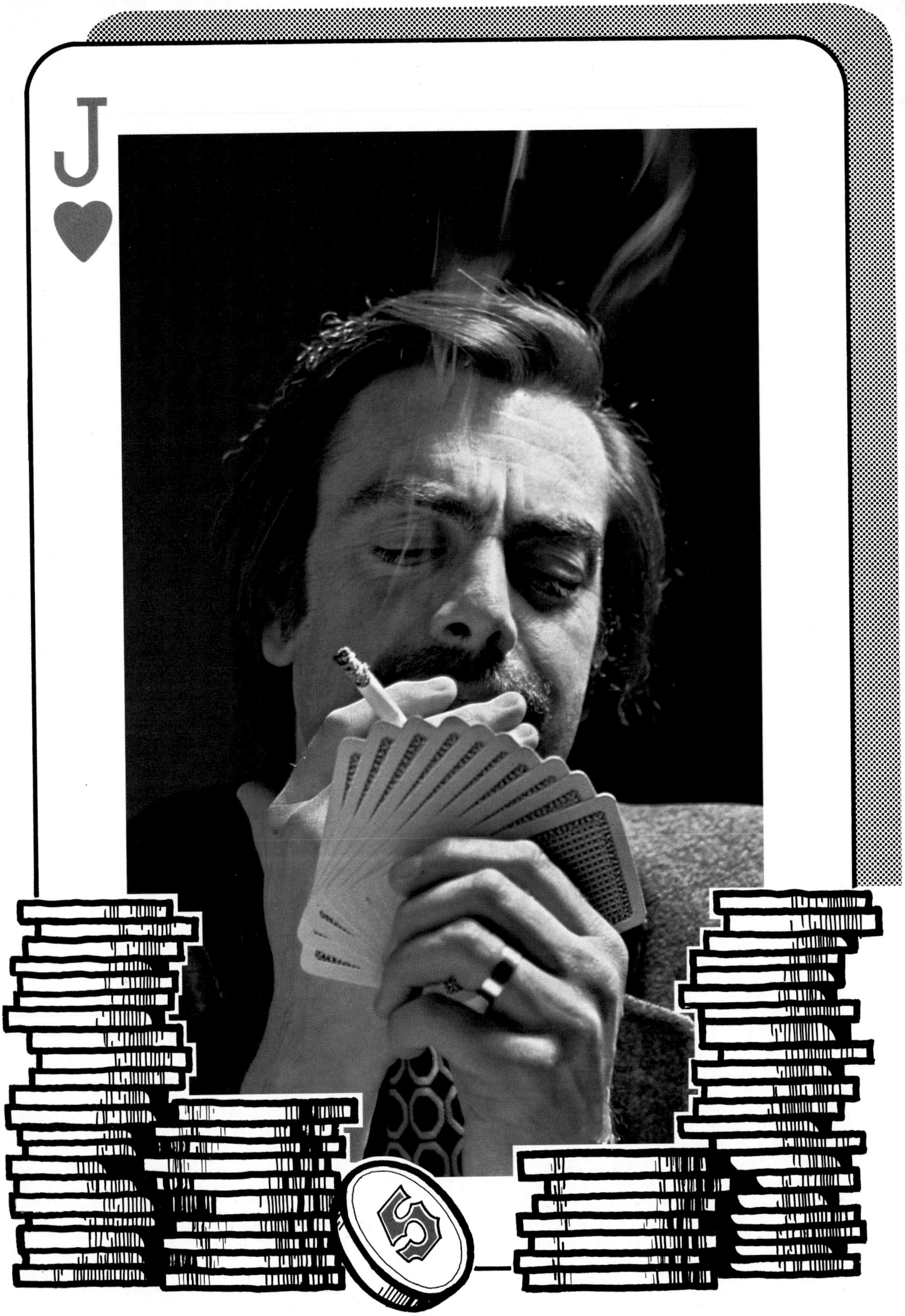

# Casino
# CARD GAMES

'He staked a fortune on the turn of a card.' This sentence crystallizes gambling. To some it suggests foolishness and irresponsibility, to others it has the same appeal as a James Bond film: there are overtones of nerve, romance, sex, the high life. In short, it means either dissipation or glamour.

The game on which the turn of a card means so much is the queen of all casino card games: baccarat.

## Baccarat
Baccarat is played in nearly all casinos. It is a simple game, very similar to *chemin de fer*. In baccarat, the bank is held either by the casino or by the highest bidder, who pays a percentage of winnings to the casino as commission. The players can be of any number, and they arrange themselves around the table shown in Diagram 4:1. When the seats are all taken, players stand behind. The banker sits in the centre, and deals only three hands, one to the players on the left, one to the players on the right and one to himself. A player may call 'banco' and bet against the whole of the bank; otherwise the players combine their stakes to equal the amount put up by the bank. The banker may not reduce the bank, and any winnings are added to it. The banker may withdraw at any time, when the bank is auctioned again.

The banker deals a card face down to the player on his right, one to the player on his left, then one to himself. He then repeats the operation. Each player represents all those on his side of the table. When one loses, the next hand is played by the next player in rotation. The object of the game is to get as near as possible to a total of nine either with the two cards dealt or with the addition of a third card

which is allowed in certain circumstances. Court cards have a value of ten; other cards represent their pip values. In assessing the total, or point, only the last digit counts; for example both 13 and 23 count as a point of 3. A point of 9 made with the two cards dealt is known as *la grande,* and a point of 8 is known as *la petite* – these hands are 'naturals' and are shown immediately. *La grande* is unbeatable; *la petite* loses only to *la grande*.

First the banker looks at his hand. If he has a natural, he turns his cards over and wins from any player who does not have a natural himself. If a player also has a natural, he will win, lose or tie according to the respective values of the two naturals. If the banker does not have a natural, he will announce that he will 'give'. The player on the right then looks at his cards. If he has a natural, he turns his cards over and wins. If his point is 6 or 7, he must stand; in other words he cannot draw a third card. If his point is 0,1,2,3 or 4 he *must* draw a third card. The player's only option in baccarat is if his two-card point is 5, when he may choose whether to stand or to draw a third card. The third is always dealt face up.

The same routine is followed with the left-hand player. The banker then has the option of either drawing a third card himself or standing, and he wins or loses to each player according to his point; if the hands are equal the stake is neither won nor lost. The banker's advantage, of course, comes from his knowledge of the player's likely point and his option of drawing or standing no matter what his own point. If the player with the larger of the two stakes against him draws a court card, the banker

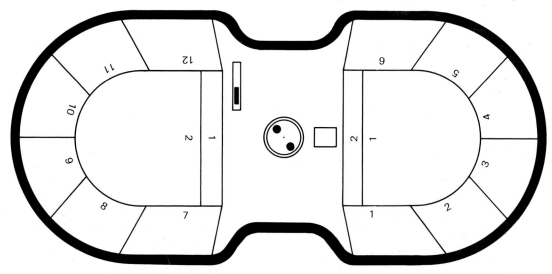

Diagram 4:1  A baccarat table

Baccarat being played in a distinguished London gaming house

knows that his point cannot be higher than 5, and can safely stand on 5 himself and be sure of not losing that stake, or on 6 and above and be sure of winning. On the other hand if the players both draw a 4, the banker knows that each player has a point of at least 4 and possibly higher and will probably draw if his own point is 5.

The cards in baccarat are dealt from a shoe or *sabot*. Six packs are shuffled and placed in the shoe, which is designed to release one card at a time. In European casinos the casino's chips are used for betting.

## Chemin de fer

*Chemin de fer* is basically the same game as baccarat, with three modifications. First of all the bank passes round the table, each player keeping it until he loses a *coup*, when he passes it on. The game is therefore suitable for private play; when played in a casino a commission is paid to the proprietors on the bank's wins. The second modification is that the bank plays against a single hand instead of two, and the third is that all options except one are removed. The rules for standing and drawing are strict and must be followed by player and banker.

The banker deals two hands of two cards each. The player who has made the highest stake plays the hand for all the players. Naturals win immediately as in baccarat. If he hasn't a natural, the player stands on 6 or 7, has the option of drawing on 5 (the only choice in the whole game) and must draw on 4 or less. The banker has no options; his actions are dictated by the rules as set out in Table 4:1.

### Table 4:1  Rules for the banker at *chemin de fer*

| If the banker's point is | He draws when giving the player | He stands when giving the player |
|---|---|---|
| 0 1 2 | 1 2 3 4 5 6 7 8 9 10 | — |
| 3 4 | 1 2 3 4 5 6 7 | 8 9 10 |
| 5 | 3 4 5 6 7 | 1 2 8 9 10 |
| 6 | 5 6 | 1 2 3 4 7 8 9 10 |
| 7 | — | 1 2 3 4 5 6 7 8 9 10 |

*Note:* If the player stands, the banker must draw if his point is 0,1,2,3,4 or 5; he must stand if his point is 6 or 7.

Hands are valued as at baccarat. The nearest point to 9 wins, except that a natural always wins over a three-card hand. Neither players nor bank win when the hands are equal.

## Baccarat–*Chemin de fer*, Nevada

In American casinos baccarat and *chemin de fer* are recent imports and the rules vary. The most popular game is a hybrid of the two: it most resembles *chemin de fer* but may be called baccarat, *chemin de fer* or even *baccarat–chemin de fer*. It may be like baccarat in that the casino holds the bank. Alternatively, if there are many players, the players may alternately hold the bank, paying the casino a commission. The wise gambler will thoroughly acquaint himself with the rules before he begins to play.

In the game described here, the most usual in Las Vegas, one hand is dealt to the players and one hand to the banker. The table used is shown in Diagram 4:2. Cards are dealt from a shoe, usually eight packs shuffled together being used. Chips are not used, the players using currency to make their bets. No options are allowed to player or bank. Naturals are declared immediately and win; if player and banker each have a natural the higher wins. The player, who is playing for all the players against the bank, must stand if his point is 6 or 7; otherwise he must draw. The banker's play is set out in the table.

### Table 4:2  Rules for the banker at baccarat–*chemin de fer*, Las Vegas style

| If the banker's point is | He draws when giving the player | He stands when giving the player |
|---|---|---|
| 0 1 2 | 1 2 3 4 5 6 7 8 9 10 | — |
| 3 | 1 2 3 4 5 6 7 9 10 | 8 |
| 4 | 2 3 4 5 6 7 | 1 8 9 10 |
| 5 | 4 5 6 7 | 1 2 3 8 9 10 |
| 6 | 6 7 | 1 2 3 4 5 8 9 10 |
| 7 | — | 1 2 3 4 5 6 7 8 9 10 |

*Note:* If the player stands, the banker must draw if his point is 0,1,2,3,4 or 5; he must stand if his point is 6 or 7.
*Variation:* In some casinos, the player may be given an option of drawing on a point of 5 and the banker may be given two options: he may stand or draw if his point is 3 and he gives the player 9, or if his point is 5 and he gives the player 4.

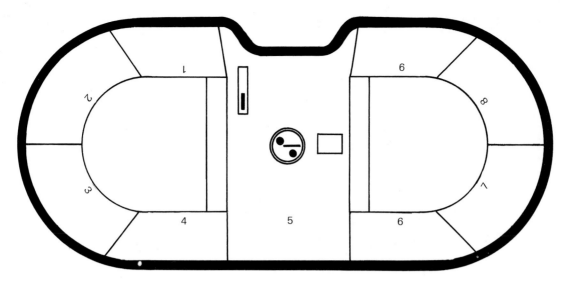

Diagram 4:2  A Nevada *chemin de fer* table.

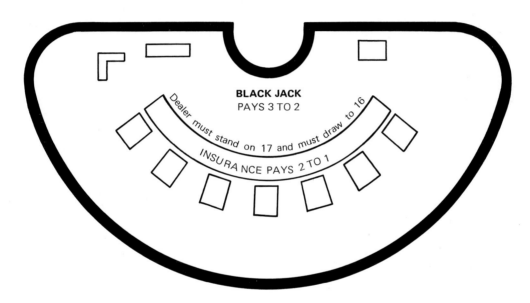

**BLACK JACK**
PAYS 3 TO 2

Dealer must stand on 17 and must draw to 16

INSURANCE PAYS 2 TO 1

Diagram 4:3  A blackjack table

In addition, side bets are allowed in American casinos (where side bets on craps are traditional). A player may back the bank to win. Since the bank (disregarding the commission to the house) has an advantage of about 1·4 per cent, a commission is levied on all such winning bets. If the commission is 5 per cent of winning bets, which is the most usual, then the percentage *against* the player backing the bank becomes just over 1 per cent.

A player may also back the banker to have a natural 8 or 9, and if successful is paid 10 for 1, or odds of 9–1. Correct odds for a natural 9 are 9·56–1, the casino's advantage in such a bet being just over 5 per cent: the correct odds against a natural 8 are slightly longer and the casino's advantage is over 6 per cent.

In the Las Vegas style of *chemin de fer* as outlined above, where no options are possible, the percentage against the player can be calculated. If he eschews the side bet of backing the banker to hold a natural, it is a little over 1 per cent, which makes it a fairer game than any other casino game with the possible exception of blackjack. A player who pays the casino 5 per cent of wins for the privilege of holding the bank (the actual arrangement varies from casino to casino) also has a disadvantage of slightly more than 1 per cent.

The player's disadvantage at *chemin de fer*, European style, is similar, but it is greater at baccarat due to the banker's additional options. It cannot be accurately estimated because in baccarat the banker is playing against two hands, and his strategy will vary according to the size of the stake on each hand.

## Blackjack

Blackjack is unique among casino games: sometimes it is actually possible for a skilful player to enjoy an advantage over the banker! Proof of this is that some casinos have found it necessary to ban consistent winners from playing. It is impossible to define the advantage precisely for two main reasons: black-

Above: Blackjack in a West London casino.　　　Opposite: A *chemin de fer* table, with a *sabot*.

A delighted gambler in a Las Vegas casino
has a blackjack

jack is a game in which there are so many options, and the rules vary considerably from casino to casino. Also it must be said that it is a game where it is not difficult to cheat and where a dealer may deny information to a player by not showing the cards when another player 'busts' and does not turn over his cards as he is entitled to do.

The rules described here are those most usually found in Las Vegas, where blackjack is the most popular casino card game.

Up to seven players sit round a table like that in Diagram 4:3. The players place their stakes in front of them and the dealer deals two rounds of cards to each player. All are dealt face down except the dealer's first card, which is face up. A single pack is used, the cards being dealt from the dealer's hand.

The object of the game is to obtain a total as close as possible to 21 without exceeding it, either with the two cards dealt, or with the addition of others which may be drawn. Court cards count as 10, Aces as either 1 or 11 at the discretion of the player, other cards at their pip values. The dealer has no options. He must draw with a total of 16 or less and continue to draw until his total is 17 or more. Once he has a total of at least 17 he must stand, and must even do so if his total includes an Ace. For instance, an Ace

and a 6 is a total of 17 (known as a 'soft' 17) and the dealer must stand; he cannot regard it as a total of 7.

This gives the player a distinct advantage. If the dealer's up-card is a 6, there is a good chance that the dealer's total is 16, since 16 of the 52 cards in the pack have a value of 10. The player may then elect to stand on 17. On the other hand, he may draw on 16 if the dealer's up-card is 7. The player may draw as many cards as he pleases.

A natural 21, known as a blackjack, is formed by an Ace and a card counting 10. This is declared immediately and wins over any other hand. When a player holds a blackjack he is paid at odds of 3–2. The dealer dealt a blackjack merely collects the player's stakes: there is no bonus.

The higher hand wins. Equal hands including blackjacks are neither winners or losers. A player whose hand exceeds 21 after drawing announces he is bust and loses immediately. Therein lies the dealer's only advantage, since he wins these bets even if he himself ultimately busts. Were the players bound by the same rules as the dealer, this advantage would give the dealer an edge of nearly seven per cent. The player's advantages already mentioned, including his bonus payout on blackjacks, reduce this percentage considerably, and skilful use of other options available to him can nullify it altogether.

One option is that if a player is dealt a pair, he may split them, that is he may regard each card as the first card of two hands, and he may double his stake, half going on each card. Many players split two 10s, but this is a mistaken policy, particularly if the dealer's up-card is 8 or 9, since an undisturbed total of 20 stands an excellent chance of winning. Were the dealer's up-card 6 or 7, it would be good play to split a pair of 8s, as 16 is a poor total, and by splitting a player may get two hands of a better value. A blackjack achieved on a split hand is paid at even money: the bonus payment of 3–2 is not made.

A second option is known as 'doubling down'. A player, after the deal, may double his stake with the proviso that he draws only one card. With a two-card total of 11, it is advisable to double down, since any one of 16 cards drawn will produce a total of 21. It is usually profitable to double down on 9 or 10, but the dealer's up-card must be taken into consideration. Were it a 10, obviously the player would not double his stake on a 9.

A player primed with all the mathematical probabilities of success on splitting and doubling-down situations, and betting accordingly, will find that blackjack is as near as possible an even game.

A third option will give him an advantage. If the dealer's up-card is an Ace, he will invite players to 'insure' against his having a blackjack. A player may back, with half his original stake, the dealer to hold a blackjack and will be paid at odds of 2–1 if he does. It is usually a poor bet. If no other cards are known but the dealer's upturned Ace and, let us say, two cards of non-10 value held by the player, then there are 16 cards left which would complete the dealer's blackjack and 33 which would not: the correct odds would be 33–16, or just over 2–1, the dealer's advantage being about 2 per cent. On the other hand, if half the pack has been used, and the player knows that there are 10 cards of 10-value remaining to 15 of non-10 value, the odds against the dealer having a blackjack drop to 15–10 and the 2–1 bet becomes a good proposition, giving the player a 20 per cent advantage.

With the rules as described, a player using his options correctly and counting the cards, i.e. keeping track of the values of the cards already dealt, can win at blackjack over a period as surely as the casino will win at all their other games.

Much work has been done recently by mathematicians on sophisticated methods of card counting, too complex for the scope of this book. Of course, when a significant number of gamblers begin to play blackjack well, and win, the casinos will alter the rules. Many casinos, in fact, already restrict the options available to players, and card counting is made more difficult in some by the use of four packs dealt from a shoe.

Blackjack is a game very much suited to sleight of hand experts and card sharps of all sorts. Casinos are undoubtedly cheated occasionally, and the less reputable ones sometimes employ as dealers gentlemen practised in the arts of crooked play. The gambler must take two precautions himself. He must know the rules of the game before he plays, and he must cease to play if anything happens to arouse his suspicions.

## Trente et quarante

*Trente et quarante* is a simple casino game popular in Europe, but rare elsewhere. The layout of the table is shown in Diagram 4:4. Gamblers have four possible bets: they may back *rouge, noir, couleur* or *inverse*, by placing their stakes in the spaces marked R, N, C or I respectively. The dealer deals two rows of cards face upwards, the first representing *noir*, the row below it representing *rouge*. With Aces counting 1, court cards as 10 and other cards at their pip value, the dealer will announce the cumulative total of the row representing *noir* as he lays out the cards and he will stop when it equals or exceeds 31. He will then do the same for the row representing *rouge*. The row with the lower total wins and backers of that row will be paid at even money.

If the first card dealt is of the colour of the winning row, then backers of *couleur* win, whereas if the first card dealt is of the opposite colour to the winning row, backers of *inverse* win. These bets are also paid at even money. If the two rows were dealt as in Diagram 4:5, *rouge* with a total of 33 opposed to 37 would win, and, as the first card dealt was the Queen of Hearts, *couleur* would win.

If the two rows have the same total, no bets win or lose, and stakes are returned, unless both rows equal 31, which is known as a *refait*. In the case of a *refait*, players may withdraw half their stake, losing the other half, or leave it 'in prison' for the next deal, when they will be allowed to retain the whole of it should it win, or lose the whole of it should it lose. The casino collects its percentage, therefore, on each *refait*. Since a *refait* occurs on average about once in 40 deals, and as the bank collects half the total stakes, its advantage over the players is approximately 1·25 per cent.

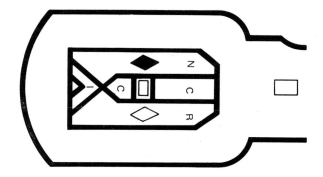

Diagram 4:4 A *trente-et-quarante* table

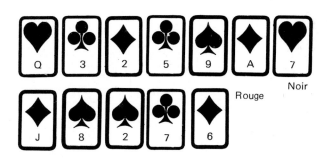

Diagram 4:5 A *trente-et-quarante* deal

# ROULETTE

## Chapter 5

Roulette is the most glamorous of casino games, and its tables attract a higher proportion of women courting Lady Luck than any others. It is not difficult to see why. The rich green baize cloth marked in red, black and gold on which the stakes are placed, the smoothly spinning wooden wheel, with its red and black compartments, the numbers in gold, the glittering silver handle by which the croupier spins the wheel, the ivory ball which clicks its way round the wheel until it comes to rest in the pocket of the winning number, together create an air of luxury, richness, sophistication and, if one is so inclined, quietly expensive vice.

Roulette is a simple game, which nevertheless provides a wide choice of bets for the gambler and allows mathematicians to devise betting systems as simple or as complicated as they fancy.

The wheel and layout as they are nowadays found in Europe differ from those usually found in America. The majority of American wheels have 38 numbers, the numbers 1 to 36, a zero and a double-zero, while the double-zero is not used on European wheels. As the odds offered are similar, the European gambler has a much better chance of winning, or at least the prospect of not losing so quickly.

Let us look first at the traditional French game. The wheel is shown in Diagram 5:1. The zero has a green background; the other numbers are alternately red and black. It is easy to arrange for alternate reds and blacks, but it is, of course, impossible to have the odd and even numbers alternate as well, as this would result in all the even numbers being either all black or all red, with the odd numbers all the same colour too. So the disposition of the numbers is arranged to space out as far as possible the odd, the even, the high, the medium and the low numbers. There are never more than two odd or two even consecutively. There are eight black odd numbers, ten black even, ten red odd, eight red even.

Stakes are placed on the table according to the layout in Diagram 5:2. The bets possible and the odds paid are as follows.

*En plein* is a bet on a single number. It is possible to bet on the zero, which in this case is regarded as just another number. The stake is placed on the number itself. The bank will pay odds of 35–1 to winners, i.e. winners will receive back 36 chips for every one staked. The correct odds, there being 37 numbers, are 36–1. The bank's advantage therefore is 2·7 per cent.

*A cheval* is a bet on any two numbers adjacent on the layout (not on the wheel). The stake is placed on the line between the two numbers. It is possible to combine the zero with 1,2 or 3. The bank pays 17–1. Correct odds are 35–2, so the bank's advantage is again 2·7 per cent.

*Transversale pleine* is a bet on three numbers. Any three in a horizontal line on the layout can be backed, such as 1,2,3 or 16,17,18, by placing the stake on the outside line opposite the three numbers, It is also possible to back zero with any pair from 1, 2 or 3. The odds paid are 11–1. Correct odds are 35–3, the advantage to the bank again being 2·7 per cent.

*En carré* is a bet on a block of four numbers, and the stake is placed on the intersection of lines in the centre of the four. It is possible, for instance, to back 26,27,29 and 30 *en carré*. Zero can be backed in conjunction with 1,2 and 3. Odds of 8–1 are paid to winners. Correct odds are 33–4 and the bank's advantage is 2·7 per cent.

*Transversale simple*, sometimes called *sixaine*, is a bet on six numbers, and this is limited to two horizontal lines on the layout, so it is not possible to back zero in a group of six numbers. An example is the group 7,8,9,10,11 and 12. Odds paid are 5–1, as against the correct odds of 31–6, with the bank's percentage remaining at 2·7.

*Colonne* is a bet on one of the three vertical columns of twelve numbers, and the stake is placed on the blank space at the foot of the selected column. The zero is *not* included in the centre column. All bets are lost if zero wins. The bank pays 2–1. Correct odds are 25–12, an advantage to the bank of 2·7 per cent. Two columns can be backed, *colonne à cheval*, at odds of 2–1 on, or 1–2. The correct odds are 13–24, and the bank's percentage is the same.

*Douzaine* is also a bet on twelve numbers. The three alternative choices are the low numbers 1–12, the stake being placed on P (for *première*), the middle numbers 13–24, the stake being placed on M (for *moyenne*), or the high numbers 25–36, the stake going on the D (for *dérnière*). Two adjoining blocks of numbers can be backed by placing the stake on the appropriate line dividing the two squares, this bet being known as *douzaine à cheval*. The odds paid, and the bank's percentage, are the same as for *colonne*.

The bets so far listed are those for which the bank pays odds of other than even money. Should zero turn up, all stakes on these bets are lost, unless of course the zero has been included in the bet. Because the odds the bank pays would be the true odds were there no zero on the wheel, it is often thought that the zero represents the bank's advantage, but this is not strictly true, since in most of these bets the zero can be backed as readily as any

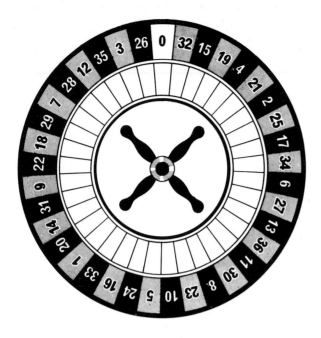

Diagram 5:1 A French roulette wheel

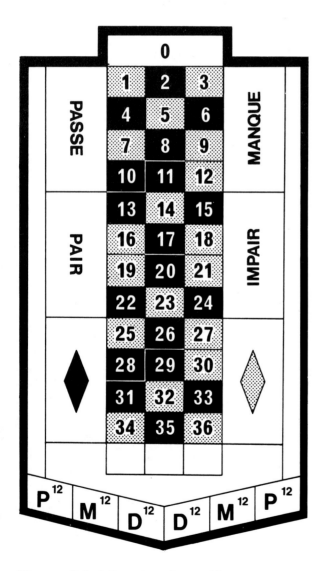

Diagram 5:2 A French roulette table

of the other numbers. Nevertheless a mistaken impression has arisen that if a bet includes zero, the bank's advantage has been nullified. As has been shown, this is not so, the bank's advantage being exactly the same, 2·7 per cent, in all these bets, whether the zero is included or not.

There remain the even-money bets, where the zero has a different characteristic. The alternative even-money bets are:

*Pair*, which is a bet on the even numbers;
*Impair*, which is a bet on the odd numbers;
*Rouge*, which is a bet on the red numbers;
*Noir*, which is a bet on the black numbers;
*Manque*, which is a bet on the low numbers 1–18;
*Passe*, which is a bet on the high numbers 19–36.
Notice that zero cannot be included in any of these bets.

If zero turns up, bets made on these even-money chances are not necessarily lost. The usual convention is for them to be put 'in prison', which means that they remain on the table for another spin. If they win on the second spin, the gambler is allowed to retain the stake, but he doesn't collect any winnings. If, on the other hand, they lose on the second spin, the stakes are lost. In effect, this is the

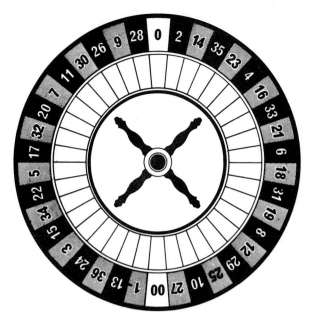

Diagram 5:3  An American roulette wheel

Roulette in the small hours in a London club

same as the player losing half his stake if zero wins, and in some casinos he is allowed to withdraw half his stake immediately and lose the other half. The effect on the bank's advantage is to halve it to a low 1·35 per cent, and it follows that mathematically the even-money bets are the most attractive. Casino practice does vary, however, and in some casinos even-money bets are lost on zero, and the bank's percentage is 2·7, as for the other bets.

If roulette in France is like a cool society beauty, in America she is a brash young lady indeed. The framework is basically the same, but some of the elegance and charm is missing and the privilege of playing costs more.

To start with, the traditional American wheel has an extra compartment marked 00, the double zero. This allows the bank to take a much bigger percentage. Wheels with a single zero are becoming more widespread in America, and money spent on gas to enable the compulsive gambler to find one is a good investment.

The double zero has led to the other numbers being positioned around the wheel in a different order. Diagram 5:3 shows the arrangement.

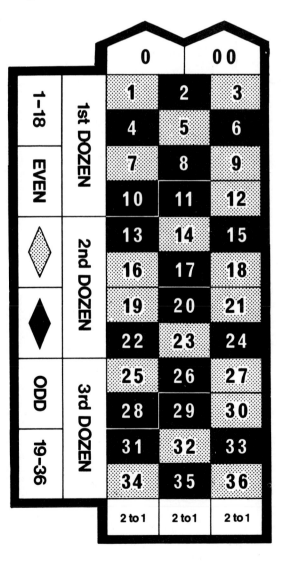

Diagram 5:4  An American roulette table

45

Opposite : A busy roulette session. Above : Elegant surroundings await the players

In two respects a consistent pattern, broken only by the zero and double zero, can be seen in this arrangement. A number on the wheel always has opposite to it a number consecutive to itself. For instance, the 1 which is next to the double zero in a clockwise direction is directly opposite 2, the 13 next to it is opposite 14, and the next number, 36, is opposite 35. Also the next red number to 1 in a clockwise direction is 36: the sum of this pair is 37. The sum of the next pair of red numbers, 3 and 34, is also 37. This convention applies to all pairs of red and black numbers all round the wheel except that the two numbers preceding the zero, red 9 and black 28, form a pair making 37, and the two numbers preceding double zero, black 10 and red 27, form a similar pair. This does not mean that the distribution of numbers on the American wheel is mathematically 'fairer' than on the French wheel, and indeed no popular systems are based on this arrangement. Each number has the same colour as it has on the French wheel, so there are eight odd and ten even black numbers and ten odd and eight even red.

The French language isn't retained in America. The croupier will probably be called a wheel roller and he will call 'No more bets' rather than 'Rien ne va plus'. The layout of the staking table is slightly different (see Diagram 5:4), but the bets and odds are nearly the same. The comparisons with the French bets are as follows.

*En plein* is known as 'straight'. Both zero and double zero can be backed. Odds are 35–1, but the bank's advantage because of the extra number (double zero) is 5·26 per cent approximately.
*A cheval* is a 'split'. Odds are 17–1, and the bank's percentage is 5·26.
*Transversale pleine* is a 'street'. Odds are 11–1; bank's percentage is 5·26.

*En carré* is a 'square'. Odds are 8–1; bank's percentage is 5·26.
*Transversale simple* is a 'line' bet. Odds are 5–1; bank's percentage 5·26. All such bets in France are on six numbers, but in America the double zero allows an extra bet, a five-number line bet on 0, 00, 1, 2 and 3. The odds paid on this bet are 6–1. The correct odds are 33–5, and the advantage to the bank on this bet is nearly 7·90 per cent.
*Colonne* is a 'column'. Odds are 2–1; bank's percentage 5·26.
*Douzaine* is a 'dozen'. Odds are 2–1; bank's percentage 5·26.

This leaves the even-money bets: even, odd, black, red, high or low. The American casino proprietor, however, unlike his European counterpart, will take all money staked on these bets if the zero or double zero wins, thereby ensuring that his advantage never drops below 5·26 per cent.

Another difference in the forms of roulette found in France and America is that in France each player's chips will be identical, and the croupier can be asked to place the stakes on the table. In America, the chips are of different colours, and each player will have his own colour. As there is no possibility of two players claiming the same stake, the players are expected to look after their own betting.

In Britain, the French wheel is used, but the arrangement of the table can follow either the French or American pattern.

A study of the most popular systems used at roulette over the years will show the variety of betting which takes place. Readers of Chapter Two will not expect any of them to provide a short cut to riches.

Simplest is the doubling-up system known as the martingale. It is usually employed on the even-money bets. Suppose the player wishes to back the odd numbers in a French casino. He will start by placing one chip on *impair*. If it wins, the punter wins one chip and that is the end of that series. If it loses, he next places two chips on *impair*. Another loss and he bets four chips, another loss and he stakes eight chips, and so on, doubling the stake after each loss. Suppose an odd number wins after four losses. The gambler wins 16 chips and on his four losing bets he has lost $1 + 2 + 4 + 8 = 15$ chips. At the end of the series he is therefore 1 chip ahead, and he begins again with a stake of 1 chip. No matter how many losses he sustains before his win, such a series will show a profit of one point. Advocates of this system sometimes suggest that the gambler should start a series when any even-money chance is 'due'; for instance he might begin backing red after four successive blacks, or odd after four successive evens. The fallacy in this line of thought was exposed in Chapter Two. It is said that the martingale system cannot lose, and indeed if the bettor had sufficient funds to double his stake *ad infinitum* it could not, were it not for one thing. Casino proprietors, knowing the danger, impose minimum and maximum limits to the stake. A usual maximum is 500 times the minimum. On a losing sequence the punter's stake will rise in the progression 1,2,4,8,16,32,64,128,256. After nine losers (and a loss of 511 chips), his next stake, 512, is not allowed, being over the maximum, so the system becomes inoperable. The probability of a sequence of nine losers is $(\frac{37}{73})^9$, roughly $\frac{1}{450}$. So, over a long run, the gambler will expect that for approximately every 450 successful series, which will net him 450 chips, he will encounter a series which will lose him 511 chips. On an American double-zero wheel he will have approximately only 320 winning series to every losing one.

It is quite possible, of course, that two gamblers, one backing red and one backing black, and both using the martingale system, will each make a profit over several hours' play on the same wheel. It is only when a long losing sequence occurs on either colour that the advantage swings back to the bank.

The martingale is unattractive to most gamblers (apart from its expected loss), as they are prepared to suffer a long series of small losses provided that occasionally they can enjoy a big win. Many prefer the reverse martingale. A gambler using this system and backing red, might place one chip on red and if it wins leave it and his winnings on the table. He might decide to do this until such time as he achieves a sequence of, say, nine winners when he will collect 512 chips as his winnings. Each time a black wins he will replace his one-chip stake. The probability of a sequence of nine wins is $(\frac{36}{73})^9$, roughly $\frac{1}{580}$. So, over a long run, the gambler will expect to lose about 580 series, costing him 580 chips, for every series

| Coup | Result | Manque Stake | Manque Position | Passe Stake | Passe Position | Bank's Position | Coup | Result | Manque Stake | Manque Position | Passe Stake | Passe Position | Bank's Position |
|---|---|---|---|---|---|---|---|---|---|---|---|---|---|
| 1 | M | 1 | +1 | 1 | −1 | — | 38 | M | 1 | +23 | 8 | −21 | −2 |
| 2 | M | 1 | +2 | 2 | −3 | +1 | 39 | M | 1 | +24 | 9 | −30 | +6 |
| 3 | M | 1 | +3 | 3 | −6 | +3 | 40 | M | 1 | +25 | 10 | −40 | +15 |
| 4 | P | 1 | +2 | 4 | −2 | — | 41 | ZERO | 1 | (+25) | 11 | (−40) | +15 |
| 5 | M | 2 | +4 | 3 | −5 | +1 | 42 | P | ↓ | +24 | ↓ | −40 | +16 |
| 6 | M | 1 | +5 | 4 | −9 | +4 | 43 | M | 1 | +25 | 11 | −51 | +26 |
| 7 | P | 1 | +4 | 5 | −4 | — | 44 | P | 1 | +24 | 12 | −39 | +15 |
| 8 | P | 2 | +2 | 4 | — | −2 | 45 | P | 2 | +22 | 11 | −28 | +6 |
| 9 | P | 3 | −1 | 3 | +3 | −2 | 46 | P | 3 | +19 | 10 | −18 | −1 |
| 10 | M | 4 | +3 | 2 | +1 | −4 | 47 | P | 4 | +15 | 9 | −9 | −6 |
| 11 | M | 3 | +6 | 3 | −2 | −4 | 48 | M | 5 | +20 | 8 | −17 | −3 |
| 12 | M | 2 | +8 | 4 | −6 | −2 | 49 | P | 4 | +16 | 9 | −8 | −8 |
| 13 | M | 1 | +9 | 5 | −11 | +2 | 50 | M | 5 | +21 | 8 | −16 | −5 |
| 14 | P | 1 | +8 | 6 | −5 | −3 | 51 | P | 4 | +17 | 9 | −7 | −10 |
| 15 | M | 2 | +10 | 5 | −10 | — | 52 | P | 5 | +12 | 8 | +1 | −13 |
| 16 | P | 1 | +9 | 6 | −4 | −5 | 53 | P | 6 | +6 | 7 | +8 | −14 |
| 17 | M | 2 | +11 | 5 | −9 | −2 | 54 | P | 7 | −1 | 6 | +14 | −13 |
| 18 | P | 1 | +10 | 6 | −3 | −7 | 55 | M | 8 | +7 | 5 | +9 | −16 |
| 19 | P | 2 | +8 | 5 | +2 | −10 | 56 | P | 7 | — | 6 | +15 | −15 |
| 20 | M | 3 | +11 | 4 | −2 | −9 | 57 | P | 8 | −8 | 5 | +20 | −12 |
| 21 | M | 2 | +13 | 5 | −7 | −6 | 58 | P | 9 | −17 | 4 | +24 | −7 |
| 22 | P | 1 | +12 | 6 | −1 | −11 | 59 | M | 10 | −7 | 3 | +21 | −14 |
| 23 | M | 2 | +14 | 5 | −6 | −8 | 60 | P | 9 | −16 | 4 | +25 | −9 |
| 24 | P | 1 | +13 | 6 | — | −13 | 61 | M | 10 | −6 | 3 | +22 | −16 |
| 25 | P | 2 | +11 | 5 | +5 | −16 | 62 | ZERO | 9 | (−6) | 4 | (+22) | −16 |
| 26 | P | 3 | +8 | 4 | +9 | −17 | 63 | M | ↓ | −6 | ↓ | +18 | −12 |
| 27 | M | 4 | +12 | 3 | +6 | −18 | 64 | P | 9 | −15 | 5 | +23 | −8 |
| 28 | P | 3 | +9 | 4 | +10 | −19 | 65 | M | 10 | −5 | 4 | +19 | −14 |
| 29 | M | 4 | +13 | 3 | +7 | −20 | 66 | P | 9 | −14 | 5 | +24 | −10 |
| 30 | M | 3 | +16 | 4 | +3 | −19 | 67 | P | 10 | −24 | 4 | +28 | −4 |
| 31 | P | 2 | +14 | 5 | +8 | −22 | 68 | P | 11 | −35 | 3 | +31 | +4 |
| 32 | M | 3 | +17 | 4 | +4 | −21 | 69 | P | 12 | −47 | 2 | +33 | +14 |
| 33 | P | 2 | +15 | 5 | +9 | −24 | 70 | M | 13 | −34 | 1 | +32 | +2 |
| 34 | M | 3 | +18 | 4 | +5 | −23 | 71 | P | 12 | −46 | 2 | +34 | +12 |
| 35 | M | 2 | +20 | 5 | — | −20 | 72 | M | 13 | −33 | 1 | +33 | — |
| 36 | M | 1 | +21 | 6 | −6 | −15 | 73 | M | 12 | −21 | 2 | +31 | −10 |
| 37 | M | 1 | +22 | 7 | −13 | −9 | 74 | P | 11 | −32 | 3 | +34 | −2 |

Diagram 5:5  The d'Alembert system in operation (see text)

Pre-war roulette in Monte Carlo

which wins 511 chips. On an American double-zero wheel he will have about 835 losing sequences for every nine-win sequence.

A more popular staking system is the d'Alembert system. It is very simple to operate. The gambler decides on an even-money bet, say *manque*, numbers 1–18. Each time he loses he increases his stake by one chip and each time he wins he reduces his stake by one chip. The intention of the system (as with the martingale) is to have the bigger bets on the winning spins. On a losing sequence the stake rises much more slowly than with the martingale system and, if one chip represents the minimum stake, the possibility of exceeding the maximum stake seems remote. It is possible to play for a very long time using this system without either profits or losses being very spectacular. Diagram 5:5 lists 74 hypothetical spins of a wheel, in which *manque* wins 36 times, *passe* 36 times and zero twice, once followed by *manque*, once by *passe*. *Manque* has winning sequences of seven and four; *passe* three sequences of four. Whichever is backed, the gambler will not need a stake larger than 13 chips. If he backs *passe*, he will at one time be 51 chips down,

Pre-war roulette in Monte Carlo

but at the end is winning 34. If he backs *manque*, he will at one time be 47 chips down. The system works to the extent that while the wheel is behaving unexceptionally, and winning and losing results remain fairly level in frequency, a small profit is likely to accrue slowly.

The systems discussed so far are based on the even-money bets. The popular Biarritz system is based on backing a single number, or sometimes three or four single numbers. It is worthless in that it is based on a fallacy. The gambler keeps a record of winning numbers for, say, 111 spins (3 × 37). In that time, according to the 'law of averages', any specified number might be expected to have won three times. If a number has not appeared in 111 spins, the theory is that it is 'due' and must appear shortly. The gambler then backs the number using a staking plan. It might be that he backs it twenty times with one chip. If it still hasn't won, he backs it twenty more times with two chips. Of course, if the number remains a 'sleeper', as such numbers are called, he is now sixty chips down and must start

staking four chips to ensure a profit should it win in the next twenty spins. Alternatively, the gambler might record the results of 37 spins and note any sleeping 'finals'. If, for instance, none of 4, 14, 24 and 34 has won, 4 is said to be a sleeping final. The gambler then backs each of these four numbers to win with a staking plan: it might be one chip each for five spins, two for the next five, four for the next five, eight for the next five, etc. It can be seen that losses mount quickly. The fallacy of the system, as readers so far will hardly need reminding, is that a sleeping number is no more likely to appear in a given number of spins than any other.

Some gamblers place much mistaken faith in a system sometimes known as the Cuban. A glance at the *colonne* bets on the staking layout will show that the centre column contains eight black numbers and only four reds. A chip placed on this column at 2–1, coupled with a chip at evens on red, means that the gambler has 26 numbers working for him, and only ten and the zero against him. If the column wins, he will win at least one chip, possibly three. If the column doesn't win, then the odds are 14–11 on red winning, as the other two columns contain 14 reds to 10 blacks (the zero making the eleventh loser). Actually the odds are slightly better, as the zero is not an automatic loser for backers of red.

However, over the long run, the *colonne* bet will lose 1 chip in 37 to the bank, the bank's advantage on this bet being 2·7 per cent. The bet on red will lose 1 chip in 73 to the bank. It is impossible to combine two losing bets to make one winning bet. In fact, the bank's advantage over players using this system is just over 2 per cent. On an American double-zero wheel the bank's advantage is 5·26 per cent.

The most interesting roulette system is the Labouchère or cancellation system. The gambler begins by writing down a series of numbers, say 1,2,3,4 or 1,1,1,1 or 2,2,2. For the purposes of illustration, let us assume a gambler has decided to back the even numbers (*pair*) and his series is 1,2,3,4. His first stake is the sum of the two outside numbers of his series, 1 and 4, so he places five chips on *pair*. If it wins, he crosses off, or cancels, the numbers 1 and 4 and backs the sum of the two outside numbers remaining, 2 and 3; his stake is again five chips. Should he win, he crosses off 2 and 3. All his numbers are now deleted, the first sequence is over and he is ten chips to the good.

Now let us suppose his first bet of five chips loses. Instead of crossing out 1 and 4, he adds his losing stake 5 to the series of numbers, so that it becomes 1,2,3,4,5. His next stake is 1 + 5 = 6 chips. The beauty of this system is that the gambler crosses out two numbers of his series for each win, and adds only one for each loss. As he is backing even chances it is clear that the series of numbers will tend to get shorter rather than longer, and every time it disappears altogether, the sequence ends with the

| Coup | Series | Stake | Win or lose |
|---|---|---|---|
| 1 | 1 2 3 4 | 5 | W |
| 2 | X 2 3 4X | 5 | L |
| 3 | 2 3 5 | 7 | L |
| 4 | 2 3 5 7 | 9 | W |
| 5 | 2 3 5 7 | 8 | L |
| 6 | 3 5 8 | 11 | L |
| 7 | 3 5 8 11 | 14 | W |
| 8 | 3 5 8 11 | 13 | L |
| 9 | 5 8 13 | 18 | W |
| 10 | 5 8 13 | 8 | W |
| 11 | 1 2 3 4 | 5 | W |
| 12 | X 2 3 4X | 5 | L |
| 13 | 2 3 5 | 7 | W |
| 14 | 2 3 5 | 3 | L |
| 15 | 3 3 | 6 | L |
| 16 | 3 3 6 | 9 | W |
| 17 | 3 3 6 | 3 | L |
| 18 | 3 3 | 6 | L |
| 19 | 3 3 6 | 9 | L |
| 20 | 3 3 6 9 | 12 | L |
| 21 | 3 3 6 9 12 | 15 | W |
| 22 | 3 3 6 9 12 | 12 | L |
| 23 | 3 6 9 12 | 15 | L |
| 24 | 3 6 9 12 15 | 18 | W |
| 25 | 3 6 9 12 15 | 18 | L |
| 26 | 6 9 12 18 | 24 | L |
| 27 | 6 9 12 18 24 | 30 | L |
| 28 | 6 9 12 18 24 30 | 36 | L |
| 29 | 6 9 12 18 24 30 36 | 42 | W |
| 30 | 6 9 12 18 24 30 36 | 39 | L |
| 31 | 9 12 18 24 30 39 | 48 | W |
| 32 | 9 12 18 24 30 39 | 42 | W |
| 33 | 12 18 24 36 | 42 | W |
| 34 | 1 2 3 4 | 5 | W |
| 35 | X 2 3 4X | 5 | L |
| 36 | 2 3 5 | 7 | W |
| 37 | 2 3 5 | 3 | L |
| 38 | 3 3 | 6 | W |
| 39 | 1 2 3 4 | 5 | W |
| 40 | X 2 3 4X | 5 | L |
| 41 | 2 3 5 | 7 | L |
| 42 | 2 3 5 7 | 9 | L |
| 43 | 2 3 5 7 9 | 11 | W |
| 44 | 2 3 5 7 9 | 10 | L |
| 45 | 3 5 7 10 | 13 | L |
| 46 | 3 5 7 10 13 | 16 | L |
| 47 | 3 5 7 10 13 16 | 19 | L |
| 48 | 3 5 7 10 13 16 19 | 22 | W |
| 49 | 3 5 7 10 13 16 19 | 21 | W |
| 50 | 5 7 10 13 16 | 20 | L |
| 51 | 7 10 13 20 | 27 | W |
| 52 | 7 10 13 20 | 23 | W |
| 53 | 1 2 3 4 | 5 | W |
| 54 | X 2 3 4X | 5 | W |
| 55 | 1 2 3 4 | 5 | W |
| 56 | X 2 3 4X | 5 | L |
| 57 | 2 3 5 | 7 | W |
| 58 | 2 3 5 | 3 | L |
| 59 | 3 3 | 6 | L |
| 60 | 3 3 6 | 9 | L |
| 61 | 3 3 6 9 | 12 | W |
| 62 | 3 3 6 9 | 9 | L |
| 63 | 3 6 9 | 12 | W |
| 64 | 3 6 9 | 6 | W |

Diagram 5:6 The Labouchère, or cancellation system in operation (see text)

Date:                                         Time:

| | 1 | 2 | 3 | 4 | 5 | 6 | 7 | 8 | 9 | 10 | 11 | 12 | 13 | 14 | 15 | 16 | 17 | 18 | 19 | 20 |
|---|---|---|---|---|---|---|---|---|---|---|---|---|---|---|---|---|---|---|---|---|
| 0 | X | X | X | X | X | X | X | X | | | | | | | | | | | | |
| 1 | X | X | X | X | X | X | X | X | X | | | | | | | | | | | |
| 2 | X | X | X | X | X | X | X | X | X | X | X | | | | | | | | | |
| 3 | X | X | X | X | X | X | X | X | X | X | | | | | | | | | | |
| 4 | X | X | X | X | X | X | X | X | X | X | X | | | | | | | | | |
| 5 | X | X | X | X | X | X | X | X | X | | | | | | | | | | | |
| 6 | X | X | X | X | X | X | X | X | X | X | X | | | | | | | | | |
| 7 | X | X | X | X | X | X | X | X | X | X | X | X | X | X | X | | | | | |
| 8 | X | X | X | X | X | X | X | X | X | X | X | X | X | X | X | X | | | | |
| 9 | X | X | X | X | X | X | X | X | X | X | X | X | | | | | | | | |
| 10 | X | X | X | X | X | X | X | | | | | | | | | | | | | |
| 11 | X | X | X | X | X | X | X | X | X | | | | | | | | | | | |
| 12 | X | X | X | X | X | X | X | X | X | X | | | | | | | | | | |
| 13 | X | X | X | X | X | X | X | X | | | | | | | | | | | | |
| 14 | X | X | X | X | X | X | X | X | X | X | X | X | X | X | X | | | | | |
| 15 | X | X | X | X | X | X | X | | | | | | | | | | | | | |
| 16 | X | X | X | X | X | X | X | X | | | | | | | | | | | | |
| 17 | X | X | X | X | X | X | X | X | X | | | | | | | | | | | |
| 18 | X | X | X | X | X | X | X | X | | | | | | | | | | | | |
| 19 | X | X | X | X | X | X | X | X | X | X | | | | | | | | | | |
| 20 | X | X | X | X | X | X | X | X | | | | | | | | | | | | |
| 21 | X | X | X | X | X | X | X | X | X | X | X | | | | | | | | | |
| 22 | X | X | X | X | X | X | X | X | X | | | | | | | | | | | |
| 23 | X | X | X | X | X | X | X | X | X | X | | | | | | | | | | |
| 24 | X | X | X | X | X | X | X | X | X | | | | | | | | | | | |
| 25 | X | X | X | X | X | X | X | X | | | | | | | | | | | | |
| 26 | X | X | X | X | X | X | X | X | X | X | X | X | | | | | | | | |
| 27 | X | X | X | X | X | X | X | X | X | | | | | | | | | | | |
| 28 | X | X | X | X | X | X | X | X | X | X | | | | | | | | | | |
| 29 | X | X | X | X | X | X | X | X | X | X | X | X | | | | | | | | |
| 30 | X | X | X | X | X | X | | | | | | | | | | | | | | |
| 31 | X | X | X | X | X | X | X | X | X | X | X | X | X | | | | | | | |
| 32 | X | X | X | X | X | X | X | X | X | | | | | | | | | | | |
| 33 | X | X | X | X | X | X | X | X | X | X | X | | | | | | | | | |
| 34 | X | X | X | X | X | X | X | X | | | | | | | | | | | | |
| 35 | X | X | X | X | X | X | X | X | X | X | X | X | X | | | | | | | |
| 36 | X | X | X | X | X | X | X | X | X | | | | | | | | | | | |

54

Above: Roulette in Cuidad Trujillo, capital of the
Dominican Republic
Opposite: Diagram 5:7 Logging 370 spins of a
roulette wheel

gambler showing a profit of the sum of the numbers in his series, in this example $1 + 2 + 3 + 4 =$
10 chips.

Diagram 5:6 shows the cancellation system in
operation over a series of results. Although in the
64 spins there were 30 winners to 34 losers, the
system operator has nevertheless managed to complete 6 winning sequences and is 60 chips in profit.

If there are $n$ numbers in the series written down,
they will all be crossed out and the sequence will be
a winning one whenever

$$W \geqslant \frac{n + L}{2},$$

W being the number of winners and L the number
of losers. In other words the sequence wins when
the number of winners becomes equal to or greater
than half the sum of the number of losers and the
number of terms in the series.

The danger comes when a long sequence is built
up with many winners which are never quite enough
to satisfy the above equation. Even in the diagram,
where the frequency of losers is never extraordinary,
stakes of 48 and 42 chips are required. The 1,2,3,4
series at these points consists of much bigger numbers and it is easy to see that a few more adverse
spins would get the numbers in the series into the
hundreds. Ten winners and twenty losers would not
be remarkable in thirty spins, but if they occurred in
an unfavourable order the stake would be well over
200 chips.

Ingenious methods have been described by which
it is alleged the house might cheat at roulette. One
involves a tiny needle which can be pushed up and
withdrawn from an imperceptible hole on the track
on which the ball is travelling; another involves
electromagnets which can be switched on at oppor-
tune times to attract a magnetized ball into a safe
pocket. Such crooked wheels are certainly made,
sold and occasionally used. Skill is required to cheat
even with such aids, as the mechanism has to be
operated at the correct split second as the wheel
slows. It would be hardly worthwhile for a
reputable casino to cheat and so place in jeopardy its
licence and the profit it makes legitimately from the
odds operating in its favour.

Roulette wheels are only man-made pieces of
equipment, subject to wear and stresses, and no
doubt many in operation have imperfections which
tend to give certain numbers on the wheel an
advantage over others. Many astute gamblers have
discovered such wheels by clocking the results over
several thousand spins. Diagram 5:7 shows how
370 results might be entered on a card. The number
370 is chosen as it shows readily how the incidence
of any number differs from the average of ten. A new
card is begun after 370 spins. It might be found that
one section of the wheel is slightly favoured, and
that one particular number wins on average once in
33 spins instead of the 'expected' once in 37. (It is
hoped, in parenthesis, that there are no 'law of
averages' advocates left among readers to suggest at
this stage that the most infrequent winning number
is backed to 'even up'.) If the favoured number is
backed and continues to win at the same rate, the
gambler has converted the 2·7 per cent house
advantage working against him into a 9·1 per cent
advantage in his favour. His object, then, is to win as
much as he can as surreptitiously as possible before
the casino realizes what is happening and changes
the wheel.

# CRAPS

Craps is essentially an American game. Of gambling pursuits probably only horse racing decides the future ownership of more American dollars than does the rolling of dice. Most money changes hands in private games, but no casino can do without crap tables. Cheating in private games is widespread, as is hustling, where innocents are relieved of their bank notes by slick operators who persuade them to take the worst of the odds. Craps is an extremely fast-moving game, where several bets can be struck and large sums change hands every minute.

The game as played in casinos is simple in principle but allows a complex variety of bets. The player, known as the 'shooter', rolls two dice across a table with a backboard from which they must bounce before coming to rest. At one time billiards or pool tables were used with a wooden rail built around them. The shooter's first roll is his 'come-out'. If the total uppermost on the dice is 7 or 11, he wins his bet. A 7 or 11 thrown on the come-out is called a 'natural'. If the come-out roll is 2,3 or 12, the shooter loses. These totals are known as 'craps'. If the shooter throws any of the other possible totals, 4,5,6,8,9 or 10, this total becomes his 'point'. To win, he must then throw his point before throwing a 7; if he throws a 7 first, he loses his bet. A 7, therefore, is a winning total on the come-out roll, but subsequently loses. A winning roll by the shooter is a 'pass'; a losing roll is a 'miss-out'.

Betting is not confined to the shooter; any player may bet before any roll. A bet that the dice will pass is called a 'right' bet; a bet that the dice will not pass is a 'wrong' bet.

There are many betting layouts. The layout in Diagram 6:1 accommodates most of the bets permissible.

Before considering the bets and their chances of success, we should look at the 36 possible ways in which the dice may fall. These are shown in Diagram 6:2.

In assessing the shooter's probability of winning on each coup, a total of 1980 hypothetical come-out rolls must be considered, as this is the lowest number which allows all possibilities to be taken into account. Table 6:1 summarizes these rolls.

Table 6:1  Shooter's probability of passing

| Come-out roll | Times thrown | Winning coups | Losing coups |
|---|---|---|---|
| Natural 7 | 330 | 330 | – |
| Natural 11 | 110 | 110 | – |
| Crap 2 | 55 | – | 55 |
| Crap 3 | 110 | – | 110 |
| Crap 12 | 55 | – | 55 |
| Point 4 | 165 | 55 | 110 |
| Point 5 | 220 | 88 | 132 |
| Point 6 | 275 | 125 | 150 |
| Point 8 | 275 | 125 | 150 |
| Point 9 | 220 | 88 | 132 |
| Point 10 | 165 | 55 | 110 |
| *Totals* | 1980 | 976 | 1004 |

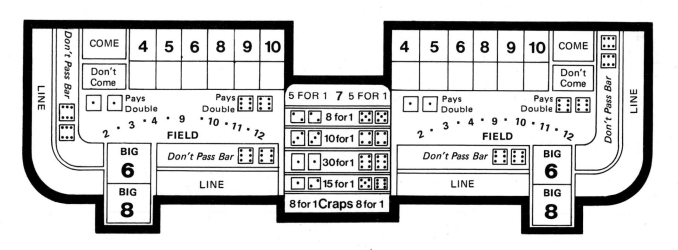

Diagram 6:1  A typical craps table layout. The 8–1 offered for double-2 and double-5, and the 10–1 for the double-3 and double-4, are hardway bets.

The 30–1 offered for double-1 and double-6, and 15–1 for 3 and 11, are one-roll action bets.

| TOTAL | NUMBER OF WAYS | ODDS AGAINST |
|---|---|---|
| 2 | 1 | 35—1 |
| 3 | 2 | 17—1 |
| 4 | 3 | 11—1 |
| 5 | 4 | 8—1 |
| 6 | 5 | 31—5 |
| 7 | 6 | 5—1 |
| 8 | 5 | 35—5 |
| 9 | 4 | 8—1 |
| 10 | 3 | 11—1 |
| 11 | 2 | 17—1 |
| 12 | 1 | 35—1 |

Diagram 6:2  The 36 ways in which two dice may fall.

Opposite: A woman shooter at a Las Vegas casino

The figures are calculated as follows. In 1980 come-out rolls, a point of 6, for example, will be thrown in the long run 275 times. To pass, the shooter must throw another 6 before a 7. As there will be six 7s for every five 6s, he will pass 125 times and miss-out 150 times.

Of the 1980 coups, the shooter can expect to win 976 and lose 1004. This represents an advantage in favour of the bank of 1·414 per cent.

In bank craps there is no private betting. All bets are made against the bank with the casino's chips and the bank takes a varying percentage.

**Win, Do, Pass or Front Line.** This is the commonest bet in casinos, bettors placing their stakes in the space marked 'line' on the layout in Diagram 6:1. It is a bet that the shooter will pass. The bank pays even money, and as has been shown enjoys an advantage of 1·414 per cent.

**Lose, Don't, Don't Pass or Back Line.** This is a bet that the shooter will lose. In the layout in the diagram, stakes are placed on the Don't Pass space. Now, we know that the shooter is more likely to lose, so to maintain its advantage over wrong bettors the bank must adjust the bet. In the layout it will be seen that the Don't Pass space carries the amendment 'Bar 6,6'. This means that if the shooter comes out with a double-6, Don't Pass bets are void, and await a further throw. Pass bets, of course, are lost. It will be seen from Table 6:1 that in the 1980

coups 55 will be double-6s. If these are deducted from the total of 1004 losing coups, there are 949 coups on which the wrong bettor will win. As there are still 976 coups on which he will lose, the bank's advantage over the wrong bettor is 1·403 per cent.

The Don't Pass bet is therefore a slightly better proposition than the Pass bet, but it is much less popular, probably because players sympathize and identify more readily with the shooter than the bank and wish him to win.

Some casinos bar double-1 rather than double-6: the percentages remain the same. However, a few casinos bar 1,2. These are to be avoided, as the bank enjoys an advantage of 4·385 per cent over wrong bettors.

**Come Bets** are made on the space marked Come in the layout. A Come bet is the same as a Pass bet, except that it is made when the shooter has already made his point. For the Come bettor, the shooter's next roll is regarded as his point. Suppose the shooter throws this sequence: 6-8-4-9-11-4-7. The shooter's point is 6, and he will lose his Pass bet when he throws the 7. A player making a Come bet before his third roll will have 4 as his point and will win when the second 4 is thrown. If he then makes another Come bet, he will win again immediately, as the 7 which loses for the shooter will be regarded as a natural for the Come bettor. The bank's advantage on Come bets is the same as on Pass bets, i.e. 1·414 per cent.

**Don't Come Bets** are the opposite of Come bets. Once again the double-6 is barred, and the bank's percentage is 1·403, as for Don't Pass bets.

**Big Six and Big Eight Bets** are made on the spaces so marked in the layout, and are bets that a 6 or an 8, whichever is backed, will be thrown before a 7. Novice gamblers might reason that a 6 can be thrown three ways: 5,1 4,2 and 3,3; similarly a 7: 6,1 5,2 4,3; and that the bet is therefore a fair one. However, reference to Diagram 6:2 shows that a 6 can be thrown five ways and a 7 six ways, so the bank enjoys an advantage of 9·091 per cent.

**Field Bets** are bets that any one of a group of numbers (in the layout they are 2,3,4,9,10,11,12) will result from the next roll. There are 16 ways these numbers can be made with two dice, as against 20 ways for 5,6,7,8. The bank's advantage would therefore be a mammoth 11·111 per cent, so the bet is adjusted by paying double on rolls of 2 and 12. This reduces the advantage to 5·556 per cent. Some banks replace the 4 in the Field with the 5. These banks do not pay double on 2 or 12, and the advantage is again 5·556 per cent.

**Hardway Bets.** The totals 4,6,8 or 10 can be made by throwing a double. A hardway bettor bets that one of these numbers will be thrown the hard way, i.e. by means of a double, before it is thrown any other way or before a 7 is thrown. Reference to the layout will show that the bank offers 8 *for* 1 on hardway 4s and 10s, and 10 *for* 1 on hardway 6s and 8s. Note that these odds are really 7–1 and 9–1. Since a 6 can be thrown five ways and a 7 six ways, and only one of these is a double 3, the correct odds for a hardway 6 are 10–1. The bank's percentage on hardway 4s and 10s is a large 11·111 per cent, and on hardway 6s and 8s 9·091 per cent. It is small wonder that casinos encourage hardway bettors. Some casinos offer shorter odds than those quoted; these casinos, or at least the hardway bets they offer, should be avoided.

**Place or Box Numbers to Win** are bets placed on one of the numbers along the top of the layout, and the bettor backs his choice to be thrown before a 7. The correct odds can easily be calculated for any number from Diagram 6:2. Table 6:2 shows the bank's percentages.

Table 6:2  Bank's percentage on box numbers to win

| Box number | Odds Bank Pays | Correct Odds | Bank's Percentage |
|---|---|---|---|
| 4 or 10 | 9–5 | 2–1 | 6·667 |
| 5 or 9 | 7–5 | 3–2 | 4·000 |
| 6 or 8 | 7–6 | 6–5 | 1·515 |
|  | evens | 6–5 | 9·091 |

59

**Place or Box Numbers to Lose** are bets that a 7 will be thrown before the chosen number, and stakes are placed in the blank box below the number selected. The bank's percentage is shown in Table 6:3.

---

Table 6:3  Bank's percentage on box numbers to lose

| Box number | Odds Bank Pays | Correct Odds | Bank's Percentage |
|---|---|---|---|
| 4 or 10 | 11–5 on | 2–1 on | 3·030 |
| 5 or 9 | 8–5 on | 3–2 on | 2·500 |
| 6 or 8 | 5–4 on | 6–5 on | 1·818 |

---

The odds 11–5 *on* means that the player *lays* the odds, i.e. the bank returns 16 chips for 11 staked, a win of 5 for the player. On numbers 4,5,9 or 10 the gambler backing the box number to lose has a better bet than the gambler backing it to win. However, it is a much less popular bet.

**Vigorish.** Some casinos will pay the correct odds on box numbers, but will exact a 5 per cent commission on winning bets. This commission is called 'vigorish'. In other casinos gamblers have the choice of paying vigorish or accepting the odds in the tables. Gamblers choosing to pay vigorish make the right choice when backing 4 or 10; on the other numbers they should take the odds offered.

**Free Bets.** When the shooter comes out on a point, most casinos allow players who have bet on Pass, Don't Pass, Come or Don't Come to double their bet, the second half of the bet being paid at the correct odds. It is called a 'free bet' and should always be accepted. The bank has no advantage on the free bet: it is designed only to speed up the action. Of course, on the total bet the bank retains an advantage, but it is considerably reduced. It is calculated as follows.

Table 6:1 shows that in the long run the bank returns to bettors on the Pass line $976 \times 2$ or 1952 chips for every 1980 staked, a profit of 1·414 per cent. It can be calculated from the table that 1320 of the 1980 come-out rolls will result in the shooter making a point, and in each case bettors on the Pass line can double their bets. If all did, the total chips staked would be $1980 + 1320$, or 3300. As the bank pays correct odds on these 1320 bets it will return 1320 chips to the players. So of the 3300 chips staked, the bank will return $1952 + 1320$, or 3272. Its advantage is therefore cut to 0·848 per cent.

The bank's advantage over Don't Pass or Don't Come bettors (as has already been shown) is normally 1·403 per cent. When the bettors take advantage of the free bet, this is reduced to only 0·832 per cent.

**One-roll Action or Come-out Bets.** Gamblers may bet on any combination appearing on any single roll of the dice, and a few of these bets are shown on the layout in Diagram 6:1. For instance a total of

Gaudy costumes and lavish decorations at a Las Vegas craps game.

7 can be backed to be thrown in any way, known as 'All 7s'. Odds offered are 5 *for* 1; correct odds are 5–1, the bank's percentage being 16·667. Odds of 30 *for* 1 are offered for double-1 and double-6. The correct odds are 35–1 and the bank's advantage again 16·667 per cent on each. Odds of 15 *for* 1 are offered for totals of 3 or 11. Correct odds are 17–1, and the percentage again 16·667. All Craps can be backed at 8 *for* 1. Correct odds are 8–1, and the bank's advantage a 'mere' 11·111 per cent. It is clear from these percentages that these bets are sucker bets. Gamblers should not be tempted by the long odds quoted for them.

**Sensible Play at Craps.** The correct odds and the bank's percentage have been given for all the common bets at craps. The player who wishes to give himself the best prospects of winning will learn them

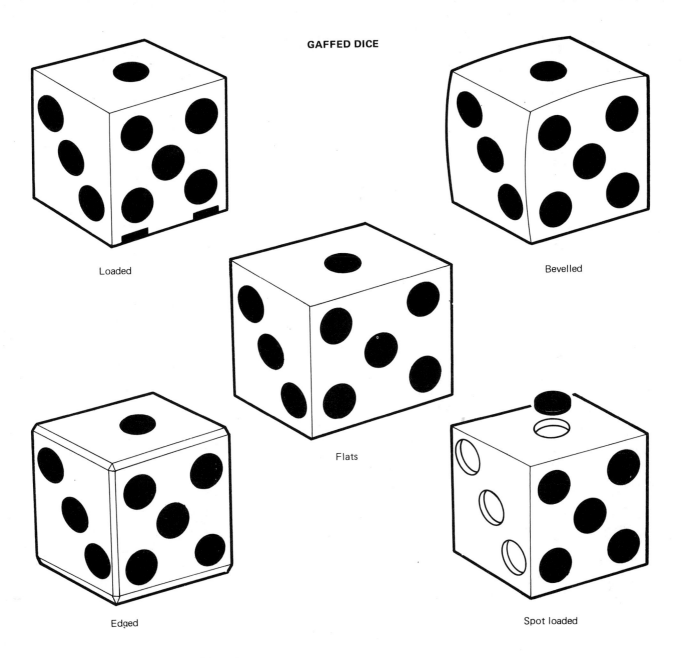

Loaded

Bevelled

Flats

Edged

Spot loaded

Diagram 6:3 Methods of gaffing dice
Opposite: Craps attracts most money in Las Vegas casinos
Below: A natural? A crap? Seconds will tell

and restrict his bets to those where the bank takes the smallest percentage. He will be wary of private crap games, where he will watch carefully for possible cheating, and where he will encounter practised players who will not only want the better half of all the bets, but will try to persuade him to concede the large percentages on the One-roll Action bets. Betting in a reputable casino is safer, because the casino's good name is worth more to it than any illegal gains.

The very best policy, then, is to bet in a good casino on the Don't Pass and Don't Come spaces and to take the free bets when available. The bank's percentage is then the lowest possible, only 0·832 per cent.

**Cheating.** Everything is done in the best casinos to prevent cheating. Officials examine the dice at every

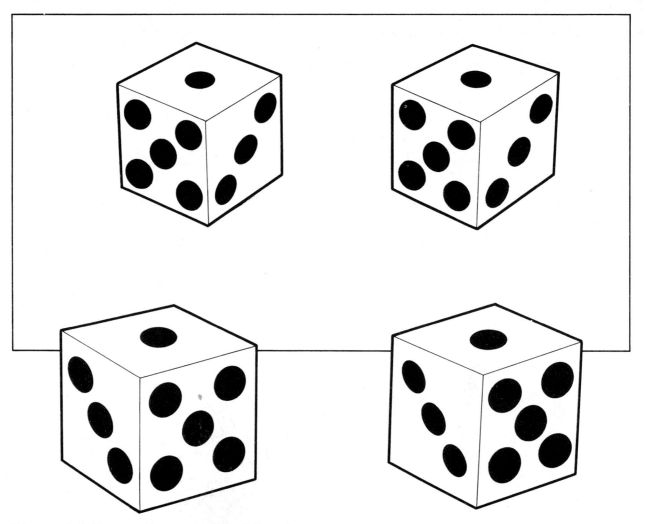

Diagram 6:4 *Tops and bottoms* reflected in a mirror

opportunity to make sure that the dice being used belong to the casino and that crooked dice have not been introduced into the game. The casino's dice are marked and the markings are frequently changed. The casino officials will also watch for attempts at controlled rolls.

Dice can be 'gaffed' in many ways. There are two basic objectives. One is to achieve a higher percentage of certain throws, either point numbers or 7s, and the other is to guarantee certain numbers. For the former dice can be:

*Loaded.* Slight weights are built into one or more sides or corners so that the opposite sides appear more often than they should.
*Bevels.* One or more sides are slightly rounded so that the dice naturally stop rolling more often on the flat sides.
*Flats.* One side is shaved so that the dice are not regular cubes and the two square sides will finish uppermost more frequently than the four rectangular sides.
*Edged.* The bevels on the edges are not cut at the same angle so that some faces are smaller than others, and more likely to finish uppermost.
*Spot loaded.* On transparent dice, minute weights are inserted behind the spots on certain faces so that the opposite faces are favoured.

Diagram 6:3 shows how these effects are achieved. Large numbers of gaffed dice are manufactured and are used freely by cheats in private games. Misshapen dice can be detected by careful scrutiny and feel. A well-known test for loaded dice is to drop a die several times into a glass of water with different sides uppermost. If the test is performed with care, true dice will fall evenly to the bottom; loaded dice will tend to turn as the loaded sides pull their way to the bottom.

One way the cheat can *ensure* that certain combinations of numbers appear is to use dice known as *Tops and Bottoms.* Only three numbers appear on the faces, the same number being repeated on top and bottom. Diagram 6:4 shows a pair of such dice. Dice with only the numbers 5,3 and 1 on them can only produce totals of 2,4,6,8 and 10. Notice that a shooter with a point of 4,6,8 or 10 cannot miss out; he *must* pass.

At this stage the sucker will laugh and claim that it wouldn't take *him* long to spot such dice. Consider two things. It is impossible to see more than three sides of a die at once. And the cheat will not use the unfair dice all the time. By sleight of hand he will introduce them only on a few favourable rolls. And if by chance a suspecting gambler picks up the gaffed dice and exposes the cheat, he will find one or two large players are accomplices.

Above: Las Vegas style craps Right: Girl croupiers bring the Las Vegas style to South London

**Dice mechanics.** Even with fair dice, 'mechanics' can perform extraordinary feats to roll certain numbers. There are two methods. The blanket roll is so called because it works well on the blanket often used as a surface in private games to prevent the dice from chipping. The dice are thrown so that they turn over like wheels, the two sides forming the 'hubs' never being uppermost. The whip shot, which takes years of practice to perfect, spins the dice so that instead of rolling they spin and slide, the desired numbers being always uppermost. Impossible though this may seem, it can be performed on the unlikeliest surfaces, and is more difficult to spot than might be thought. Gamblers should always suspect unconventional rolls or throwing actions, and should leave any game where every aspect is not patently above-board.

## Chapter 7

# Famous
# CASINOS

The Société des Bains de Mer et Cercle des Etrangers (the Sea Bathing Society and Circle of Foreigners) sounds more like a multi-national beach party than a gambling organization, but it is in fact the society which owns the Monte Carlo casino. It was formed by François Blanc in 1863.

François and his twin brother Louis made money as stockbrokers in Bordeaux but, as it was made through bribing telegraph workers, it earned them a spell in prison. On their release they opened a casino in Luxembourg, and later operated one in the Bavarian state of Homburg. Meanwhile, an unsuccessful casino was operating in Monaco. When in 1861 France annexed most of Monaco, what was left of the principality was more of a rock than a country and Prince Charles was forced to look to the casino as a principal source of revenue. The French were persuaded to build a railway from the prospering resort of Nice, and François Blanc (his brother had died) was asked to take over the casino. Blanc went further: he began to build a town around the casino. The town grew till it nearly *was* Monaco, and it was called Monte Carlo in honour of Prince Charles.

Blanc was immediately successful. The new railway, the boom on the Riviera, which became a popular holiday area for rich Americans as well as the European aristocracy, and Blanc's astuteness in cutting the casino's percentage and thereby increasing business, all contributed to undreamt-of prosperity for Blanc, the casino, Monte Carlo and Prince Charles.

Monte Carlo has style. It has received glamorous publicity ever since the Prince of Wales became an habitual visitor in the last years of the nineteenth century. Although not a flamboyant gambler, he rarely missed a season for thirty years and brought social status to the casino. The resort became fashionable as other rulers arrived: Kaiser Wilhelm II, King Leopold II, Emperor Franz Josef and Czar Nicholas II among them. Sarah Bernhardt and Eleonora Duse, the great actresses, liked to gamble: the divine Sarah too much. After one particularly distressing loss, she tried to commit suicide. If the resultant publicity spotlighted the dangers of the lure of the casino, the activities of Charles Wells in 1891 really hit the promotional jackpot and established Monte Carlo as the world's most famous casino. In a dazzling run of luck, Wells broke the bank at one of the roulette tables. At that time, each table started with a bank of 100,000 francs. Camille Blanc, the son of François, who had died in 1877, was by now running the casino, and he made the most of his misfortune by making sure Wells' feat became well known, draping the table with black

Opposite: Monte Carlo, Las Vegas and Reno at night
Above: The Monte Carlo casino's own school for croupiers

crepe. Wells' astonishing run continued, and he broke the bank again and again. He left Monte Carlo having made over a million francs. Charles Coborn sang a song based on Wells in a revue. Called 'The Man Who Broke the Bank at Monte Carlo', it swept the world. There was speculation about Wells' system, but he later admitted that he had none, and that his win was extraordinary luck. Wells lost all his money on a later expedition to Monte Carlo and was imprisoned for losing other people's too. He died a poor man, having provided the best publicity any casino ever had.

A man who did employ a system and won was William Jaggers, who studied the roulette wheels until he discovered an imperfect one which favoured certain numbers. He, too, won over a million francs before the casino discovered his method and corrected the bias.

After the First World War, Monte Carlo faced competition from casinos on the French Riviera, and it was necessary to re-establish its supremacy. Elsa Maxwell, the professional party-giver, was

Above: The Monte Carlo casino in 1874
Left: Elsa Maxwell, Monte Carlo party giver

asked to revitalize the social life. Soon, not only was royalty to be met again, but successful business men like André Citroën and Gordon Selfridge became familiar figures at the tables. The late Aga Khan was a frequent visitor; show business people flocked there; the chronicler of the twenties, Scott Fitzgerald, was at the parties; Winston Churchill holidayed there.

The casino continued to operate during the Second World War, but another saviour was required soon afterwards, as it began to lose money. He arrived in the person of Aristotle Onassis, who bought the Sea Bathing Society and rejuvenated Monte Carlo. His yacht, *Christina*, was usually in the harbour, on board statesmen, industrialists, artists, film stars and the great opera singer Maria Callas, whose attachment to Onassis kept Monte Carlo in the world's newspapers for months. In 1956 Prince Rainier married the beautiful American film star Grace Kelly. Two thousand writers and photographers made sure the wedding was not unnoticed. A century after its opening, the Monte Carlo casino, commanding the principality from its position high up on the rock, retains its aura of opulence and glamour, a playhouse for the rich and famous.

Inside, the casino does not quite live up to the splendour of its reputation. The big gambling takes

Above: Aristotle Onassis and his yacht *Christina*
Right: Prince Rainier and Princess Grace at a
Monte Carlo gala

place in the *salles privées;* tourists fill the smaller
rooms, known collectively as 'The Kitchen', where
the grandeur is missing and first impressions usually
disappointing. The casino uses its own chips or
plaques, different colours representing varying
denominations, and employs its own police force and
security guards. Croupiers are trained at the casino's
own school. The games played are mainly roulette,
baccarat, *chemin de fer* and *trente et quarante*. Craps
was added in 1949 to satisfy the increasing numbers
of American visitors, and there are now even slot
machines.

The early success of Monte Carlo led to com-
petitors. Casinos were built in the leading French
resorts once public gambling was allowed by the law
in 1907. The biggest French casinos are at
Deauville and Cannes. The casino at Deauville was
founded in 1912 and is now a complex which contains a huge restaurant, a cinema and a theatre.
Nico Zographos and the Greek Syndicate did much
to make Deauville and Cannes famous, winning
millions of francs in the twenties and thirties from
gamblers like André Citroën, Solly Joel and the
Duke of Westminster.

Nice, from whence in the nineteenth century the
railway took gamblers to Monte Carlo, now has
flourishing casinos of its own. Le Tourquet and

Left: The casino at Monte Carlo
Above, left: Roulette at Las Vegas
Top: Slot machines at the Desert Inn, Las Vegas
Above: Craps at the Circus, Circus, Las Vegas

Left: *Chemin de fer* at a London card club
Right: William Crockford, founder of
Crockford's Club

Biarritz in France, San Remo, Venice and Rome in Italy and Estoril in Portugal, also provide green-felt scenery where the wheels turn and the dice rattle.

The casino at Homburg, which François Blanc created before he developed Monte Carlo, closed in 1872, and pride of place among German casinos belongs to Baden-Baden. Dostoevsky gambled at Homburg right up to its end, and also at Wiesbaden and Baden-Baden, although it was at Saxon-les-Bains that the advance on *The Gambler* was dissipated at roulette. Baden-Baden has achieved its eminence comparatively recently. The casino has been in existence for 200 years, but it was the health-giving waters which attracted most nineteenth-century visitors.

In London in the eighteenth century, gambling was one of the main attractions at the select clubs, particularly Brooks's and White's, in St James's Street. The members, who included statesmen, nobility and the mere idle rich, entered their wagers in a book, and bets were made on racehorses, the imminence of wars, which countries were liable to invade which others, the life expectancy of older members and the prospects of certain unmarried ladies (not named – the bettors were always gentle-men) producing children by given dates. William Crockford, the son of a Temple Bar fishmonger, and a passionate gambler and bookmaker on the race-course and in the sleazy taverns around Temple Bar and the Strand, was aware of the exclusive world of the clubs and nursed a desire to belong to it. An untidy fat man, with a coarse cockney voice and an insatiable appetite for women and food, Crockford seemed unlikely to be accepted by the society to which he aspired, but he made sufficient money on the racecourse by devious means to buy four houses in St James's Street, which he knocked down to

build a gambling club of his own. He also had to help re-build the neighbouring Guards' Club, which the zeal of his workmen had caused to fall down. Nevertheless, in 1828, Crockford's Club opened. The Duke of Wellington, the Earls of Sefton and Chesterfield and Prime Minister Disraeli were early members, the Club became fashionable, the profits mounted, and soon William Crockford, fish-monger's son, was living in Carlton House Terrace as the proprietor of the most renowned gambling house in the land. His remaining ambition was to win the Derby and he owned the second favourite, Ratan, in 1844. This notorious race was won by an ineligible 4-year-old (see Chapter Ten), and Ratan, who was suspected of being doped, finished seventh. Three days later the disappointed Crockford died, claiming with his last words that he had been 'done'. Crockford's death coincided with a strict enforce-ment of gambling laws, and a year later the club was closed. The building was later the home of the Devonshire Club, and Crockford's house in Carlton House Terrace was sold and eventually belonged to Prime Minister Gladstone. However, in 1928, exactly 100 years after the opening of the original Crock-ford's Club, the name was revived for a bridge club, and with the betting acts of the 1960s the gaming traditions were also revived and today 'Crockford's' is once more a gambling club.

The new laws led to the existence of over a thousand gaming clubs in Britain. It was evident that many were becoming haunts of criminals, and that 'protection money' was being paid by pro-prietors. The lessons of the early Las Vegas days

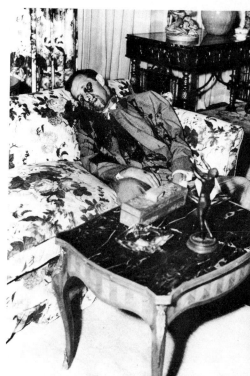

Left: Croupiers practising at England's first casino
of the 1960s at Brighton
Right: The end of Bugsy Siegel

were heeded, and stricter licensing laws were introduced by the Gaming Act of 1968. The novelty of
casinos, which had led to an initial boom among
gambling-starved Britons, declined at the same time,
and today a hundred or so clubs satisfy the late-
night bettor's needs.

New Orleans has pioneering status in American
casino life. As filmgoers know, the Mississippi
paddle-boats were almost floating casinos, in-
complete without a suave card manipulator. The
town was already a gambling centre when John
Davis in 1827 (the year Crockford's was being built
in London) decided to attract gamblers with a classy
decor and good food and drink: it was an early
recognition that customers are willing to lose more
money if the surroundings are luxurious. This was
America's first 'carpet joint'. Nowadays, the most
ostentatious carpet joints exist in Nevada. Casinos
in other states are illegal and tend to be functional
'sawdust joints'.

Las Vegas is now the world's largest gambling
centre, gambling having been legalized in 1931.
However, it took more than the 1931 law to change
this small town in the Nevada desert with a few
thousand inhabitants into the Temple of Mammon
it is today. To be precise it took a gangster of vision
to do it: 'Bugsy' Siegel, dope pusher, rapist, boot-
legger, robber and wholesale murderer by contract.

Siegel's associates were Al Capone, Dutch Schultz,
Vito Genovese, Lucky Luciano, Frank Costello,
Meyer Lansky, leaders of the Mafia and other
notorious gangsters. Crime was a business. Before
1946 Siegel was building up a successful fleet of

gambling ships operating three miles off the Southern
California coast. Governor Warren nipped this
operation in the bud. Siegel rightly decided that if
people would go out to ships to gamble, they would
be willing to travel to the desert. On Boxing Day,
1946, he opened in Las Vegas the fabulous Flamingo
Hotel, a several million dollar investment comprising
a casino, theatre, restaurant, pool, lawns and
gardens, where the best black-market materials
ensured that no facility or convenience was missing.
Bugsy ruled it all like a film star playing a gangster:
handsome, immaculately groomed, with pin-striped,
wasp-waisted suits, hand-made shoes, silk mono-
grammed shirts and fat cigar. Bugsy once had a
house in Beverly Hills and mingled with the stars.
George Raft was a particular friend and admirer.

The Flamingo flopped at first. After two weeks
it closed and did not open again for three months.
Meanwhile Bugsy's relations with Al Capone and
the Mob became strained. Bugsy had built up the
Trans-America wire service, giving racing information to illegal bookmakers for the Capone gang.
When the owner of the rival Continental Press
Service was rubbed out, Capone owned this too, and
wanted to disband Trans-America. Siegel wouldn't
co-operate. In June 1947, just as the Flamingo was
beginning to flourish, he was shot dead as he sat in
the Beverly Hills mansion of his mistress. Slugs from
a carbine fired through a window smashed him up.
A card pinned to the newspaper he was reading
said, 'Good night. Sleep peacefully with the compli-
ments of Jacks's.' As with the twelve murders Bugsy
himself claimed to have committed, nobody was
convicted. Gus Greenbaum, who became Mayor of
Paradise, and claimed Al Capone and Senator Barry
Goldwater as friends, later took over the Flamingo,
and made a $4 million profit in his first year.
Greenbaum, too, eventually disappointed the Mob,

Opposite: Blackjack tables at Las Vegas          Above: Classy decor at a Las Vegas carpet joint

Below: Al Capone, underworld influence on Las Vegas casinos
Right: Monte Carlo casino interior, 1893

and when he and his wife were found with their throats cut Goldwater was at the funeral.

The publicity of these murders did nothing to halt the boom. In 1950 the Desert Inn opened. It was built by the ever-smiling Wilbur Clark, another ex-Mayor of Paradise, but largely financed by Sicilian gangsters from Cleveland. The Desert Inn was followed by the Sahara, the Sands, the Stardust, the Dunes, the Tropicana. The Stardust was run by gangster Tony Cornero, who died in the Desert Inn while playing craps. A few years earlier he had recovered from being shot in the stomach. Cash accounts of the Tropicana were found in the pocket of Sicilian gangster Frank Costello when he was shot in the face in New York in 1957. The most famous Las Vegas casino owner was singer Frank Sinatra, who sold his interests for $3½ million in the 1960s. Sinatra owned a large share of the Cal Neva Lodge, and 9 per cent of the Sands, where the strident floor shows and loud music usual in the other casinos

Frank Sinatra, erstwhile casino owner

took second place to his own smooth reassuring voice issuing from all the speakers. Mafia leader Sam Giancana stayed at Cal Neva Lodge in 1963 despite being banned from casinos by a Nevada State Gaming Board black book, and the investigations and publicity surrounding this incident may have decided Sinatra to give up gaming. Shortly afterwards Sinatra had to pay a $240,000 ransom to get back his son, kidnapped from a Nevada casino where he had a singing engagement.

Las Vegas at this time was a remarkable place, and one of its remarkable characters was Father Crowley, the 'gambler's priest'. He would conduct mass in the early morning for croupiers, punters and the whole gambling circus in the Stardust casino. When he left Las Vegas, he sold his Mercedes (a gift) and attended an all-night party given in his honour, where he did a soft-shoe shuffle.

The visitor to Las Vegas casinos today sees no sign of the crime by which they were built. The accent is on luxury and the materialistic good life. The city worships money. The man with the most is the king. A big loser is admired as a 'spender'. On the 'Strip', the main highway, are the casino-hotels, with their bars, country clubs, swimming pools, golf courses and restaurants. There is a lack of windows and clocks; the gambler is cocooned in an unending atmosphere of the big-time. Beautiful women and piles of money are in attendance, usually attending to each other. In Glitter Gulch, around Fremont Street, are the sawdust joints, with names like Horseshoe, Lucky Strike and Jackpot, where there are rows and rows of one-armed bandits. All interests are catered for, provided they are gambling, drinking or fornication. Few people take away from Las Vegas more money than they arrived with. It is a monument to the gambling urge and to gamblers' eternal optimism.

# HORSE-RACING

## Chapter 8

According to Homer, after the Trojan war the victorious Achilles arranged games as part of the funeral ceremony for his friend Patroclus, killed by Hector. The first event was a chariot race. Antilochus was given his riding instructions by the wise Nestor, who had perhaps walked the course in advance. However, Eumelus, the Lester Piggott of the day, led in the first furlong, and his mares were going easily when divine intervention by Pallas Athene broke the yoke of his chariot and he fell. Idomeneus, an early bookmaker, saw what had happened, even without binoculars, and quickly offered odds to Aias about Eumelus's prospects and these were accepted. Diomedes of the loud war cry won in a driving finish from Antilochus, who just pipped Menelaus for second place. Menelaus promptly objected to Antilochus for crossing. The winner's prize was a delightful woman and a tripod holding twenty-two pints. The second received a mare in foal.

Men have matched horses for speed all over the world, and gambled on the result. It is interesting that this early race contained all the elements that have fascinated followers. The best horseman was robbed by dirty work on the part of the Gods. There was an argument over rough riding, and an objection. The winner got the girl and the booze. The loser was left to raise another horse to fight another day. And, last but not least, the crafty bookmaker cleaned up.

Racing is one gambling pursuit where the winning of bets is not the only measure of success or means of pleasure. Apart from the whole business of owning, breeding and training horses, and the prestige of winning the famous races, immense satisfaction is gained by all followers from the spectacle of a great horse. Champion racehorses inspire tremendous affection, and a meeting of champions in a great race provokes speculation and excitement in people who would regard betting on the outcome as almost blasphemous.

In Britain, the great flat races are the five Classics (the 1000 Guineas, the 2000 Guineas, the Derby, Oaks and St Leger, all for three-year-olds). There are other important races, particularly at Royal Ascot and the principal Goodwood meeting, both of which are social occasions, and at Newmarket, the headquarters of British racing. Over the sticks in winter, the most famous race is the Grand National, perhaps the toughest in the world. It is a vast betting medium, but, being a handicap, is rarely won by the best horse in the field. The real champions stake their claims at Cheltenham, where the Gold Cup for steeplechasers and Champion Hurdle are run.

Only three Classics are open to colts, the 1000 Guineas and Oaks being reserved for fillies. The treble of the 2000 Guineas, Derby and St Leger is known as the Triple Crown. The last horse to perform this feat was Nijinsky in 1970, the previous Triple Crown winner being Bahram, owned by the Aga Khan, in 1935. One filly, Meld, has won the 1000 Guineas, Oaks and St Leger since the war: her great year was in 1955. In 1942 Sun Chariot achieved this treble in wartime substitute races for King George VI. Royalty has always supported the 'sport of kings'. Charles II was frequently at Newmarket, where the Rowley mile course perpetuates his nickname of Old Rowley, and the present Queen and Queen Mother have owned good horses, the best being Aureole and the most famous the Queen Mother's Devon Loch, who fell on the flat when certain to win the Grand National in 1956. King Edward VII, when Prince of Wales in 1900, became the only owner to win both the Derby and Grand National in the same year, and his horse Diamond Jubilee won the Triple Crown. The aristocracy have a traditional association with the Turf, the Derby being initiated by Lord Derby and Sir Charles Bunbury, and indeed the race might easily have been the Bunbury, as the two men tossed for the honour of naming it.

Recent equine heroes in Britain have been the contemporaries Mill Reef (owned by American Paul Mellon) and Brigadier Gerard, the Derby winner Sir Ivor, the great hurdlers Persian War and Bula, and the famous Arkle, who in many minds replaced Golden Miller as the greatest steeplechaser

Opposite: The Grand National, 1971.
Above: Parade for the Stewards' Cup at Goodwood

ever. Top jockey is Lester Piggott, but Sir Gordon Richards, with more British winners than anybody in history, is a living legend.

Thoroughbred racing in America (where harness racing is also popular) is quite unlike racing in Britain. To start with, it is illegal in many states. Consequently there isn't a national authority like the Jockey Club (the American Jockey Club has limited power). In the states where it is allowed racing is conducted by a Commission, and a National Association of State Racing Commissioners meets to exchange information. It also attempts to standardize rules. The courses are usually circular dirt tracks unlike the undulating grassland of British courses. American race-tracks are more concerned with the spectators' comfort. The British racegoer usually enjoys pleasanter, more natural surroundings; the American racegoer enjoys superior facilities, more information and a better view of the whole race.

Race-tracks get much more use in America. The biggest track in the world, Aqueduct, near New York, and its neighbour Belmont Park, stage some two hundred days' racing a year. Meetings might last a month or more, whereas four days is the norm for an important meeting in Britain. These two tracks and Saratoga Springs are the main ones for New Yorkers.

Laurel Park, Maryland, is famous throughout the world for the Washington International race, in which horses from Europe, Australia, Russia and Japan have been invited to participate since its inception in 1952. The Preakness Stakes is also run in Maryland, at Pimlico. There are five major race-tracks in California, and as one meeting ends another starts, so that racing takes place during most of the year. In all, there are about thirty-five major tracks in America, and a hundred or so smaller ones.

America has its Triple Crown: the Kentucky Derby, the Preakness Stakes and the Belmont Stakes. Perhaps the most famous American race-horse is Man O'War, successful both on the track, where he was beaten only once, and at stud. His

Arkle winning the Whitbread Gold Cup

A driving finish in an American race

racing days were just after the First World War. More recent American giants were Native Dancer and Kelso, who won the Washington International in record time in 1964, and a total of nearly two million dollars in stake money. Eddie Arcaro and Johnny Longden are the best-known jockeys.

Racing in France is more like American racing than British. It is concentrated on Paris, where racing takes place for most of the year at Longchamp. Maisons-Lafitte, Evry and Chantilly are other courses for Parisians. Chantilly is just outside Paris, and is the headquarters of French training and the home of the Prix du Jockey Club, the French Derby. In August the racing scene shifts to Deauville, a seaside resort. These are the big French meetings, but smaller meetings take place all over the country. Big French races are run on Sunday, a blank day in Britain.

French racing has been organized on business-like lines in the last few years. All betting takes place on the *pari mutuel*, and over 10 per cent of the pool is ploughed back into racing. Longchamp has become one of the most beautiful courses in the world, and its principal race, the Prix de l'Arc de Triomphe, is arguably the world's most important race. The leading French jockey is Yves St Martin, but nowadays

the French racegoer can regularly see the best British and Australian jockeys riding against the more dynamic home products. Champion French horses include Tantieme, who won the Prix de l'Arc de Triomphe in successive years in 1950 and 1951, Vaguely Noble, who won the Arc and won in England, Exbury, who also won in England, and the great Sea Bird II, who won the English Derby and the Arc, both in brilliant style.

Australians are famous for a predilection for gambling and a fondness for horses. It is not surprising that horse-racing is something more than popular. Australian jockeys usually have a quiet style and are good judges of pace; many of them have ridden with great success in Europe or America, notably Rae Johnstone, Scobie Breasley and George Moore. There are several hundred courses in Australia, and not unnaturally the more important are in the bigger towns. Melbourne is perhaps the biggest centre and stages the Melbourne Cup at Flemington and the Caulfield Cup at Caulfield. Melbourne, Sydney and Brisbane all have three or four courses.

Hurdling at Cheltenham, with, inset left, flat racing·in America and, inset right, the paddock at Chantilly

Above: The American race-horse Man O'War
Below: Sir Gordon Richards, left, and Johnny
Longden, after swapping headgear

Bookmakers are being replaced by the tote in Australia, particularly in off-course betting, and as in France a percentage of the profit is given back to the sport, and is used to improve the racing and the facilities.

Racing in New Zealand is conducted on the same lines as in Australia, the principal track being Ellerslie, near Auckland. However, the best horses usually make their reputations in Australia, and New Zealand horse-racing bears a relationship to Australia's similar to that between Ireland and England. Both New Zealand and Ireland, with their lush grasslands, are great breeding grounds for horses, many of which are sold to their larger neighbours.

A legendary Australian racehorse, Phar Lap, was bred in New Zealand. He won 37 races, including the Melbourne Cup, before dying mysteriously while on a tour of Mexico and America. Phar Lap can be seen at Melbourne, where he stands in a glass case at the museum.

On the Continent, racing is popular in Germany, Italy, Belgium and Scandinavia, as well as in France, and perhaps Italy takes pride of place, because of two world-famous horses. Nearco was the first and he had a brilliant career on the course, and at stud, where his line includes important winners in Europe and America. Rome and San Siro, near Milan, are the centres of racing in Italy, and it was at San Siro that Ribot, whom many consider the greatest of all racehorses, first established his reputation. He was unremarkable to look at, but was unbeaten, winning all the important Italian races as well as the Arc de Triomphe twice and the King George VI and Queen Elizabeth Stakes at Ascot. Retired to stud in 1957, Ribot has sired Ribocco, who won English and Irish classics, Molvedo, who won the Prix de l'Arc de Triomphe, Arts and Letters, the great American champion, and other good horses.

Racing is popular in South Africa, despite an unhelpful climate, and Wilwyn, the first winner of the Washington International, is at stud there. The principal tracks are around Durban, Johannesburg and Cape Town. South African horses rarely travel abroad, but jockey John Gorton, who came to England in 1969, soon demonstrated that he was of the highest class.

British flat-race jockeys sometimes ride in India in the close season, and no doubt British rule did a lot to establish racing there. Bombay and Calcutta are the main centres.

Racing takes place on a comparatively small scale in Russia, where all horses are owned by the State. Betting is through the tote. Russia sent Zabeg to finish third in the 1960 Washington International and Anilin to finish second in 1966, so the standard is respectable.

The country which owns the fastest-growing racing industry is Japan. There are five principal meetings, at Tokyo, Nakayama, Hanshin, Chukyo and Kyoto. The boom has come since the Second World War, and Japan has modelled its racing on that of France. Betting is high, and takes place on the tote, a percentage of the proceeds being ploughed back into the sport. Japanese buyers have been

Vaguely Noble, winner of the Prix de l'Arc de Triomphe

buying mares and stallions from Europe in large numbers over the last few years, and although no Japanese horse has yet made a mark in international races, the quality of the horses is improving fast.

It is clear that racing flourishes best in those countries like France and Japan where all betting is on a *pari mutuel* basis, with a percentage being taken for the improvement of the industry. Bookmakers, although they contribute to the colourfulness of racing as a whole, particularly in Britain, might be regarded as an expensive anachronism. Britain is now the only major racing country in the world not working towards a tote monopoly. Money is ploughed back into the industry via the Horserace Betting Levy Board, which since 1968 has exacted a levy on bookmakers (and the tote) based on their turnover. Between 1961, when the Board was formed, and 1968, when the Government taxed betting, the levy was based on bookmakers' profits. The money put back into racing in those years was considerably less than the sum French racing received from the *pari mutuel*, with the result that France became the centre of European racing.

From the gambler's point of view, there is a big difference between betting with the tote, or *pari mutuel*, and with the bookmaker. The tote is a pool into which all stakes are placed. After deductions, i.e. expenses, tax, etc., there is a sum left which is divided among the winners. (In practice, there is more than one pool on each race: there may be, for instance, win, place, and forecast pools; in America, there may be win, place and show pools.) Consequently, when making their bets, gamblers do not know how much to expect if they win, since the total pool is being increased right up to the time of the race, as is the number of tickets on each horse. At race meetings, 'approximate odds' boards are displayed, but of course the odds fluctuate as the betting continues.

There are two principal ways to bet with bookmakers. If the gambler is betting ante-post (i.e. striking a bet about a future race) or on the course, he will accept an agreed price and will be paid out accordingly if he wins. For instance, if 20–1 is accepted about a winner, that is what the gambler will be paid irrespective of whether the odds change subsequently.

Opposite, above: The field round Tattenham
Corner in the 1972 Derby at Epsom
Opposite, below: Virginia Boy winning the
Wokingham Stakes at Royal Ascot, 1970

Above: Triple Crown winner Nijinsky, with Lester
Piggott up, after his King George VI and Queen
Elizabeth Stakes win, Ascot, 1970
Right: Bookmakers on Oaks Day at Epsom

Most betting with bookmakers in Britain, however, takes place at starting price. Bets made in
betting shops on the day of the race will be executed
at starting price (unless otherwise arranged). The
official starting price is determined by a small
group of men at the course (representatives of the
*Sporting Life* and *Sporting Chronicle*) who take the
average of the bookmakers' prices being offered at
the 'off'. Considering the amount of money at stake,
this method seems haphazard and obviously open to
corruption. It is astonishing, and says a good deal for
the integrity of the men involved, that thousands of
starting prices are returned each year and accepted
without question.

Let us look first at the bets which are available on
the tote. Bets on the tote are made not on the
horse's name, but on its number on the race card.
In Britain, every horse can be backed to win on the
tote, irrespective of the number of runners. There is

no place betting with five or fewer runners. If there are six or seven runners, a horse can be backed for a place, which means it must finish first or second. The place bet is a separate transaction to the win bet: a bettor backing a horse for win and place will receive two tickets. Both tickets can be bought at the same tote window, but windows vary according to the amount to be staked. The units are of 10p, which is the minimum stake and the stake to which dividends are declared. If there are eight or more runners, a horse needs to finish in the first three to obtain a place.

If there are three to six runners, a straight forecast pool is also run. Bettors are required to name the first two horses to finish, in the correct order. If there are seven to ten runners, a dual forecast pool is run, in which the bettor backs two horses to finish first and second in either order. Should an outsider win from the favourite, the dividend paid for the dual forecast is likely to be less than the dividend paid on the winner alone. The dual forecast dividend in this case would obviously have been the same had the favourite won from the outsider. This is not the case, of course, in straight forecasts.

The tote also runs daily double and daily treble pools. The daily double is based usually on the third and fifth races on the card. The gambler buys a ticket on a horse in the third race and, if it wins, exchanges it for a ticket on a horse in the fifth race – should this win too he collects the dividend. The tote treble is based on the second, fourth and sixth races. A recent innovation on the tote is the introduction of the jackpot pool. This is operated at the principal meeting of the day on most days of the season. Backers are required to name the winners of all six races, or of the first six if there are more than six on the card. Should nobody win the pool, as sometimes happens, it is carried forward to the next jackpot meeting, after a consolation dividend has been paid to backers of the first five winners. Astute gamblers will realize that this presents them with a bonus, since the pool on the second day will be greater than the total stakes: in theory it is possible that the 'percentage' will (for once) favour the backers. In fact this is well realized and if, say, £5,000 is carried over to the second day, the pool is likely to swell to, say, £50,000. The tote's commission and tax will then cancel out the favourable edge, but even so the bet on a carried-over jackpot is a much better bet than gamblers can usually obtain.

In 1973 the Tote Board began a new pool, the Roll-up administered by the Pools Promotors Association (to which British football-pool companies belong). In thirty or so special races throughout the season (races with sixteen runners, there being reserves to substitute for withdrawn horses), gamblers are asked to name the first six horses to finish in the correct order. Because this is extremely difficult (there are 5,765,760 possible forecasts of the first six of sixteen runners) the dividends are high. As with the Jackpot, the pool is carried over to the next race should it not be won, and an early winner of a carried over pool collected over £70,000 for the standard 5p stake.

In Britain, where bookmakers provide an alter-

Above: Tanino Moutiers winning the Japan Derby at Fuchu
Below: Australian-born jockey Rae 'Togo' Johnstone rode mostly in France, but is here in the Royal purple, scarlet, gold braid and black velvet

native method of backing a horse, it is frequently better to prefer the tote when backing outsiders in large fields (where the bookmakers usually lump outsiders together as, say, '33–1 others', odds which are often much shorter than the true ones) or when backing 'unfashionable' stables or jockeys, who tend, for some reason, to be ignored by tote backers, the dividends consequently being higher.

Betting on the American tote is slightly different. A horse can be backed to win only, or it can be backed for a place, which means it must finish first or second, or it can be backed to show, which means it must be first, second or third. A bet on all three – backing a horse to win, place and show – is known as a combination bet, or a bet across the board. In Britain, a bet that a horse will win or be placed is known as an each-way bet. The tote also operates a quinela bet, which is the equivalent of the British dual forecast: the bettor names two horses to finish first and second in either order. There is also a daily double, usually operated on the first and second races, but sometimes on another pair of races.

The number of tickets is restricted to twelve on the American tote, so if there are more than twelve runners in a race, two or more are bracketed together, or sometimes the outsiders are bracketed together as 'the field'.

On the French *pari mutuel*, horses in the same ownership are bracketed together. This is a convention never used in Britain, but it is a good system, because whenever a backer finds his horse beaten by a longer-priced horse in the same ownership, he is inclined to shout 'fix'. This cry from the pocket can be silenced for ever by the simple adoption of the French system.

The most popular bet with French punters is the *Tiercé*, an off-course pool similar to the British Tote Roll-up. Each Sunday, and sometimes on other days, a race is selected, usually a large-field handicap, and bettors are asked to name the first three in the correct order. Consolation dividends are paid to those who pick the first three in the wrong order.

In Britain, the amount of betting handled by bookmakers is several times that handled by the tote.

Betting on big races starts with the ante-post book. On races such as the Derby, prices will be advertised in the newspapers before the season begins, and there will usually be a well-defined winter favourite. The odds quoted are 'all-in, run or not', which means that the backer loses his money if the horse is scratched before the race. Prices are therefore on the generous side. Bookmakers claim that they sometimes make no profit on the ante-post book. One need not suspect philanthropy from this unlikeliest of quarters: the gain is in prestige and advertising. On the ante-post book, a professional backer, or one with stable connections, can make profits. If he knows a horse is being trained for the race, he might obtain 50–1 several weeks beforehand. The odds might contract to 10–1 just before the race, when the backer can 'lay off' all or part of

Discussing an Ascot victory are trainer
Noel Murless, owner Stanhope Joel and jockey
George Moore

Opposite: The paddock after the Melbourne Cup    Above: Mill Reef winning the 1971 Derby      Below:
Mill Reef's great rival Brigadier Gerard,  Joe Mercer up, after a Prince of Wales Stakes win, Ascot, 1972

Newbury on February 10, 1973, in which there were five runners. In Table 8:1 the odds against each horse are converted to probability percentages.

Table 8:1   A bookmaker's percentage

| Horse | Odds (starting price) | Odds converted to percentage |
|---|---|---|
| Golden Reppin | 7–4 | 36·36 |
| Dick Owen | 15–8 | 34·78 |
| Echo Sounder | 3–1 | 25·00 |
| Bramwell Boy | 8–1 | 11·11 |
| Cabro | 25–1 | 3·84 |
| | | 111·09 |

This table shows that if each horse were backed with a sufficient stake to enable the backer to get back 100 units from the bookmaker whichever horse won, the backer would require 111·09 units as stakes and would lose 11·09 units on the race. It might be said, therefore, that the bookmaker's edge is 11·09 per cent on the starting price. Bookmakers would argue, justifiably, that backers on the course can place their bets when the odds are favourable to them, i.e. most of the horses would at one stage of the market fluctuations have been on offer at odds longer than the eventual starting price. They might have been shorter, too. This argument works both ways.

The bookmaker's percentage of 11·09 quoted above is average for a five-horse race. On the same day at Newbury, in the big race, a 26-horse handicap, the bookmaker's advantage was nearly 39 per cent. On top of these percentages, the lucky gambler in Britain must pay tax on his winnings. Bookmakers are taxed and pass it on to winners at about 5 per cent. This emphasizes the advantage of betting on the tote in big fields.

One drawback of the British starting-price system which perturbs punter and bookie alike is the weakness of the course market. A large bet on the course can influence the odds disproportionately. The 'blower' system counteracts this in some measure. The 'blower' is the name given to a company which transfers bets from bookmakers' offices to the course, thus ensuring that bookies do not face huge liabilities over horses which start at a false price because of limited course betting. This subject is referred to again in the chapter on frauds. Bookmakers use this system to their advantage. If a bookie accepts in his office a huge bet on a horse offered on the course at 20–1, he can transfer it whole or in part to the course, which might bring the odds down to, say, 6–1. If the horse wins, he pays out his client at 6–1, but is paid himself at odds up to 20–1. Of course he cannot do this if his client's bet is struck at an agreed price, as an ante-post bet would be, which is why it is more difficult for a bookmaker to balance his ante-post book.

A quick arithmetical brain and a knowledge of the theory of probabilities are of limited use to the racing

Above: Runners and riders board at now-defunct Hurst Park
Opposite, above: Remarkable triple dead-heat at Melbourne, 1956
Opposite, below: Diagram 8:1. How a course bookmaker keeps his book. The first column under each name is a running total of the bookmaker's liability on the horse, the second column records each bet, the third column is a running total of the stakes on each horse, the fourth column is the ticket number. For example, the holder of the last ticket issued, No. 147, has taken £22 to £8 on Water Wheel, bringing the total stakes on that horse to £116 and the liability to £426

his bet (known as hedging), and be in pocket whatever the result.

On the day of the race, bookmakers will accept bets at starting price, and backers will have their stakes returned in the case of a late withdrawal.

Unlike the tote, bookmakers can lose on a race. They must endeavour to quote odds so that their liabilities on all the runners can be balanced and a profit made whichever horse wins. In fact, this ideal state isn't always achieved, and most bookmakers are prepared to accept a loss occasionally if the favourite or another fancied runner wins. However, to see how a book can be balanced, let us look at the starting prices of an actual race – the Compton Chase at

| Robin Hood | | | | | Stretchford | | | | | Rhino Rose | | | | | Water Wheel | | | | |
|---|---|---|---|---|---|---|---|---|---|---|---|---|---|---|---|---|---|---|---|
| | 30 | 10 | | 113 | | 20 | 20 | | 111 | | 30 | 5 | | 115 | | 50 | 20 | | 116 |
| 60 | 15 | 5 | 15 | 118 | | 20 | 20 | | 112 | 49 | 12 | 2 | 7 | 119 | 77 | 5 | 2 | 22 | 120 |
| | 70 | 20 | | 122 | | 10 | 10 | | 114 | | 16 | 2 | | 123 | | 25 | 10 | | 126 |
| 195 | 35 | 10 | 45 | 125 | | 20 | 20 | | 117 | 112 | 40 | 5 | 14 | 124 | 126 | 10 | 4 | 36 | 127 |
| | 30 | 10 | | 132 | 240 | 50 | 50 | 120 | 121 | | 80 | 10 | | 130 | | 11 | 4 | | 128 |
| | 15 | 5 | | 135 | | 20 | 25 | | 129 | 257 | 50 | 5 | 29 | 134 | 291 | 110 | 40 | 80 | 131 |
| 275 | 15 | 5 | 65 | 138 | | 40 | 50 | | 133 | | 50 | 4 | | 142 | | 55 | 20 | | 140 |
| | 70 | 20 | | 139 | | 50 | 50 | | 136 | 365 | 50 | 4 | 37 | 146 | | 22 | 8 | | 141 |
| | 35 | 10 | | 143 | 515 | 20 | 20 | 265 | 137 | | | | | | 426 | 22 | 8 | 116 | 147 |
| 500 | 70 | 20 | 115 | 144 | 605 | 40 | 50 | 315 | 145 | | | | | | | | | | |

**25p** TREBLE EVENT **25p** 6

DO NOT DESTROY THIS TICKET
UNTIL THE DIVIDEND IS DECLARED.

CODE HORSE

1ST LEG

**50p** **Place** **50p** OC

CODE RACE HORSE

**50p** TEAY 3•01

**tote** ISSUED SUBJECT TO RULES OF THE
HORSERACE TOTALISATOR BOARD
163, EUSTON ROAD, LONDON, N.W.1.
ENTRANCE IN UPPER WOBURN PLACE

D 081032 5C

ONE POUND **WIN** **£1** 130

CODE RACE HORSE

**£1** TEAY 3•01

**tote** ISSUED SUBJECT TO RULES OF THE
HORSERACE TOTALISATOR BOARD
163, EUSTON ROAD, LONDON, N.W.1.
ENTRANCE IN UPPER WOBURN PLACE

D 095364 £1

FIVE POUNDS **Forecast**

CODE RACE

**£5** EAY 7•2

**tote** ISSUED SUBJECT TO RULES OF THE
HORSERACE TOTALISATOR BOARD
163, EUSTON ROAD, LONDON, N.W.1.
ENTRANCE IN UPPER WOBURN PLACE

**50p** DAILY DOUBLE **50p** 17

IF THE HORSE No. PERFORATED BELOW IS THE WINNER, EXCHANGE THIS
TICKET PRIOR TO THE ADVERTISED TIME OF THE NEXT APPOINTED RACE

CODE RACE HORSE

ROVE 3•17

RETAIN THIS TICKET
UNTIL THE "WEIGHED IN"
IS SIGNALLED

L 045288

DAILY 1ST LEG DOUBLE

ONE HORSERACE TOTALISATOR BOARD ONE
163. EUSTON ROAD. LONDON N.W.1
**25p** **JACKPOT** **25p**
UNIT UNIT

SERIAL No. C197301 SERIAL No.

ENTER YOUR SELECTIONS HERE

CLIENTS
COPY
KEEP USE RACECARD
NUMBERS
THIS ONLY
COPY

ISSUED SUBJECT TO TOTALISATOR RULES GOVERNING THIS POOL
C O D E

**KEEP THIS COPY**
ALWAYS RETAIN THIS TICKET UNTIL DIVIDEND IS
DECLARED. VALID DAY OF ISSUE ONLY.

ONE HORSERACE TOTALISATOR BOARD ONE
163. EUSTON ROAD. LONDON N.W.1
**25p** **JACKPOT** **25p**
UNIT UNIT

SERIAL No. C197301 SERIAL No.

ENTER YOUR SELECTIONS HERE

RACE ONE USE RACECARD
RACE TWO NUMBERS
RACE THREE ONLY
Do RACE FOUR
NOT RACE FIVE
FOLD RACE SIX

ISSUED SUBJECT TO TOTALISATOR RULES GOVERNING THIS POOL
C O D E

**PLACE THIS COPY IN SPECIAL
BOX BEFORE THE OFF OF RACE ONE**
VALID DAY OF ISSUE ONLY

*JOE CORAL LTD.*
Head Office :
252 - 260, REGENT STREET,
— LONDON, W.1. —
(BETTING DUTY NO. 17710003)
*'Never a Quarrel - Bet with Coral'*

**B** **B** CIVILTY

P.P.W. LTD., 207 Dalston Lane, London, E.8.
FOUR FIVE FIVE

*JOE CORAL LTD.*
Head Office :
- 260, REGENT STREET,
— LONDON, W.1. —
(BETTING DUTY NO. 17710003)
*'Never a Quarrel - Bet with Coral'*

**B** CIVILTY

P.W. LTD., 207 Dalston Lane, London, E.8.
FOUR FIVE SIX

Derby Day, 1972. If finding winners is
difficult, what about an ice-cream, a soft drink,
a ride on the roundabouts or a flutter at bonanza
bingo?
Opposite: British tote tickets and course bookmaker's
tickets

Photofinish to the 1949 Derby. Nimbus (Charlie Elliott) wins from Amour Drake (Rae Johnstone) and Swallow Tail (Doug Smith)

man. First requisite for betting success is a knowledge of stable opinion. It is not always true that all horses in a race are both fit and trying. It is widely believed by punters, rightly or wrongly, that horses are sometimes given easy races so that the handicapper, who allots the weights they carry, will under-rate them in future events. This is absolutely illegal and will lead at least to suspensions if discovered. On the other hand it is acknowledged that a horse not quite at peak fitness is sometimes given a 'warm-up' race. With horses, like jockeys, entitled to 'off' days, it is impossible to be sure that all horses in all races are running honestly. Betting coups are attempted, and landed, on unlikely horses all too frequently for any realist to believe that there is no shady work on the racecourse. The racegoer and the racing press implicitly accept this fact, and 'fancied' is sometimes a tipster's euphemism for 'trying'.

Considering the sums of money involved, racing is more honest than anybody could reasonably expect. It is conducted with considerable publicity, and stewards and journalists are ready to pounce on any suggestion of crooked practice. In America, the Thoroughbred Racing Protective Bureau keeps an enormous black-list of dubious characters, and stamped out 'ringing' (the substitution of one horse for an inferior one) by instituting a system in 1945, whereby all horses have an identification number tattooed on their lips.

A second route to punting success is a close study and correct interpretation of the form book. Details of all horses' past performances are readily available.

Summaries of form for each day's racing are published in the specialist press and in all the British national newspapers. Racegoers take for granted the daily paper service, and seldom reflect on the amount of racing space and information their few pence buy them. The best American racing paper, the *Morning Telegraph*, contains even more information than the British press.

When comparing the performances of race-horses, it is usually reckoned that one length equals 3 pounds of weight over sprint distances and perhaps only 1 pound over 2 miles. Additional allowance must be made for horses which win 'cleverly', i.e. those horses which do no more than is necessary to win; for horses which are running over a distance not their best; for horses running on going which they dislike; for horses unlucky in the running; and for horses with any other mitigating circumstances or excuse. Some experts rely entirely on race times. Most gamblers who bet for recreation rely on form or hunches, but it is a very skilful bettor who can beat the bookmaker's percentage and the tax for any length of time.

The number of betting systems in use is almost as high as the number of gamblers using them. Staking plans are popular, but must always be unsatisfactory in some degree because the odds vary from race to race: it is impossible to base a staking plan on even-money chances, say, as one can in roulette.

The 'blower' service. The women in the foreground are connected directly to the course, those behind accept bookmaker's instructions

Systems must depend on a gambler's pocket and inclinations. Whereas some are based on logic, others are not, and it seems reasonable to reject the latter, at least.

A well-known adage is 'fourth in the Guineas, first in the Derby'. This may have produced winners in the past, but it is illogical to believe that the fourth horse in the 2000 Guineas has a good Derby chance merely for this reason – it is not a system which bears examination.

Backing the outsider of three runners is a popular system. It may be that intense wagering on two evenly-matched horses leads to the third being un-reasonably neglected, but it is a slim psychological theory on which to risk good money.

When a jockey is lighter than the weight which his horse has been set to carry, the weight is made up by the insertion of leads in the saddle. Some punters like to back jockeys who are riding at their natural weight. The premise is that a horse whose burden is all muscular jockey will run faster than one carrying lumps of lead, particularly over a long distance. It sounds likely enough: the system is recommended.

Most newspapers indicate those horses who are running at meetings a long distance from their stables. To back these is logical: presumably trainers do not go to the expense and trouble of sending horses on long journeys unless they fancy their chances.

Following winning two-year-olds until they lose also has the merit of reason. A two-year-old who has won has shown that he has learnt how to race and he has not had much time to develop a dislike of the sport, so he will often win again.

Backing horses on their names, or numbers on the race-card, or on coincidences like Easter Hero running on Easter Monday is needless to say a short cut to bankruptcy. Other systems with as little to recommend them are frequently dressed-up with science. It is often said that professional gamblers back four or more horses in a race and 'amateurs' are advised to do the same. But to back four horses per race indiscriminately does not reduce the bookie's edge at all. He will love clients who take this advice. Systems for staking are often presented with much mumbo-jumbo – one article of several hundred words in a racing paper boiled down to advice to the reader to put his biggest stakes on winners and smallest on losers, which seems to beg a question!

There is one good system which applies to all others, and that is not to use a system without testing it. Two tests might be applied. First, is it based on a reasonable premise? So many systems are based ultimately on whim or fancy and this test will enable them to be discarded immediately. Secondly, do past results support the system? A small sum spent on the books which list past races season by season and a few hours spent applying the system to them will, in theory, show whether the system has much chance of success in the future.

| | |
|---|---|
| erby | Leeds |
| AN. CITY OR NDERLAND | Luton |
| Wolves | Coventry |
| verton | Sheff. Utd. |
| an. Utd. | Newcastle |
| orwich | Leicester |
| outh'pton | Birmingham |
| toke | Liverpool |
| ston Villa | Portsmouth |
| lackpool | Fulham |
| ristol C. | Oxford Utd. |
| ardiff | Burnley |
| arlisle | Orient |
| udd'field | Middlesbro |
| illwall | Preston |
| heff. Wed. | Brighton |
| windon | Nott'm F. |
| lackburn | Swansea |

# Football
## POOLS

Association football began in Britain in the nineteenth century, and betting on it no doubt started practically at once. Today football pools are popular in many parts of the world, but Britain still claims the highest number of top-class teams and players, and the biggest football-pools industry.

Football pools are the main gambling pastime for many Britons. About 12 million punters stake nearly £200 million every year, usually in the hope of landing a jackpot prize of £500,000. The largest pools company, with over half the total business, is Littlewoods Pools Limited.

Littlewoods was started in 1923 by John Moores, who invested £50 in the project. The first coupons were distributed by hand outside Manchester United's ground. The punters totalled 35, and the stakes were £4. 7s. 6d.

Most football-pools betting is carried on by post, although since the 1950s the companies have also been using collectors, area agents who call at homes collecting the coupon and the stakes and delivering the following week's coupon. There is a choice of pools on each coupon. The most popular pool is the Treble Chance, where from a list of about 54 English and Scottish League or Cup games, clients are asked to select eight matches to end in a draw. The number of selections required and the method of scoring have changed often over the years. The current system is that a score-draw (one in which each side scores) counts 3 points, a 0–0 draw counts 2 points, a win for the visiting side $1\frac{1}{2}$ points, and a home win 1 point. The maximum score is therefore 24 points (eight correctly forecast scoredraws) and in most weeks 24 points will win lucky punters several thousand pounds for a 1p stake. It should be noted in this context that there are 1,040,465,790 different ways of choosing 8 matches from 54, and that if only 8 matches result in scoredraws there is only one chance in that number of choosing them. The Littlewoods pool pays six dividends, so that clients with only 21 points usually can expect a very small win.

Another pool is the 12-Match Points Pool, where the client is asked to forecast the outcome of the week's twelve most evenly balanced matches. The punter marks against each match 1 for games he thinks will end as home wins, 2 for away wins and X for draws. He is allowed 3 points for a correct draw forecast, 2 points for an away and 1 for a home. If in a particular week the 12 matches result in 4 draws, 2 aways and 6 homes, there is a maximum of 22 points, and clients with an all-correct line will receive a substantial dividend. Clients with 21 and 20 points will receive consolation dividends.

Other pools require the punter to select either four draws, four aways or eight results from the full list of matches. Most people choose eight home wins when betting on the 8-Results Pool, since home wins are commonest and easiest to forecast.

The total stakes on any one pool are returned to the winners, after deductions have been made for the pools company's expenses and profits and government tax. These deductions are huge. The government takes $33\frac{1}{3}$ per cent of stakes in taxes. Although pools companies take only about 3 per cent of the pool as profits, their expenses in the form of wages, rents, printing, commission to collectors, etc. amount to about another 25 per cent. The punters, then, will get less than half their stake money returned to them in the form of winnings, making football pools just about the worst gamble invented. Their popularity depends on the prospect they offer of a really big win. A man winning £50,000 for 1p is hardly likely to rue the fact that a 'fair' return would have been £100,000.

In the immediate post-war years, newspapers popularized pools 'permutations'. Each paper had a regular column by an expert. Perms allow bettors to make systematic multiple bets.

Full perms are popular. A man betting on the Four Aways pool may fancy six away teams to win. He can back any combination of four from these six by entering 2 against all six matches and then writing alongside 'Any four from six = 15 lines at 10p = £1.50 staked'. This is a full perm. If any four of the matches are away wins he will win a dividend; if any

Brothers John (left) and Cecil Moores, heads of Littlewoods

Charles 'Ginger' Baker shared a cheque from Vernons Pools for £154,199 with three co-punters in 1973

**Diagram 9:1** A four-aways full perm

**Diagram 9:2** The 15 lines in full

### 12 MATCH POINTS POOL 3 DIVS

CORRECT FORECASTS SCORE HOME 1 pt. AWAY 2 pts. DRAW 3 pts.

MARK 1 for HOME / 2 for AWAY / X for DRAW

| | | | |
|---|---|---|---|
| Carlisle | Sheff. Utd. | 1 | 2 X |
| Chelsea | Ipswich | 2 | 1 X |
| Oxford Utd. | Q.P.R. | 3 | 2 X |
| Sheff. Wed. | Crystal P. | 4 | 1 X |
| Wrexham | Walsall | 5 | 1 X |
| Bury | Southport | 6 | 1 X |
| Darlington | Gillingham | 7 | 2 X |
| North'pton | Lincoln | 8 | 1 X |
| Peterboro | Mansfield | 9 | 2 X |
| St. Mirren | Partick | 10 | 1 X |
| Stirling A. | Arbroath | 11 | 1 X |
| Stranraer | S.Johnst'ne | 12 | 2 X |

ALLOW FOR UP TO 3 DRAWS 299 LINES AT 1p £2·99 STAKED

Min. 1/4 Per Stake 4p Line. Max. Per Stake 1 1p Line

**Diagram 9:3** A 12-match points pool perm

five he will win five dividends; if all six he will win 15 dividends. The entry is shown in Diagram 9:1 and the 15 separate lines are shown in Diagram 9:2.

A punter might select on the 12-Match Points Pool the team more likely to win each match. He might then feel confident that any nine of his 12 forecasts might prove correct, but might wish to insure himself with the other three. Perhaps one, two or three of his selected teams might only achieve a draw and not a win. He could then use the entry in Diagram 9:3. He will have 1 line representing his twelve selections without a draw, 12 lines containing one draw, 66 lines containing two draws (any combination of 2 from 12 = 66), and 220 lines containing three draws. The perm is a method of backing 299 separate entries without the necessity of laboriously writing out 299 lines of selections.

A simple perm for the Treble Chance is shown on the right in Diagram 9:4. If any three matches from each of groups A and B and any two matches from C result in score-draws, the punter will have an all-correct line winning a first dividend. If all twelve selections are score-draws, he will have 36 first dividends.

Pools companies make perms even easier these days by issuing booklets of perms before the season starts. The perms are identified by numbers. For example, the Littlewoods coupon in Diagram 9:4 contains two black columns, A and B. A punter

wishing to use, say, Lit-Plan 83, which is set out in full in the booklet, merely enters X against the necessary 16 selections in Column A, ticks the appropriate box and returns the coupon with the 90p stake. This perm has been entered in the diagram.

To cover all 16 of the selections in a full perm (any 8 from 16) would take 12,870 lines. Lit-Plan 83 consists of 180 lines, and carries a guarantee. The 180 lines are worked out so that if eight of the 16 selections are score-draws, there will be at least nine lines containing six of them, or one line containing seven or eight. If ten of the 16 matches are score-draws, at least six lines will contain seven of them.

Littlewoods celebrated their golden jubilee in 1973: fifty years of continuous growth. By the outbreak of the Second World War, the total staked per week had risen from the £4. 7s. 6d. of the first coupon to nearly half a million pounds. After the

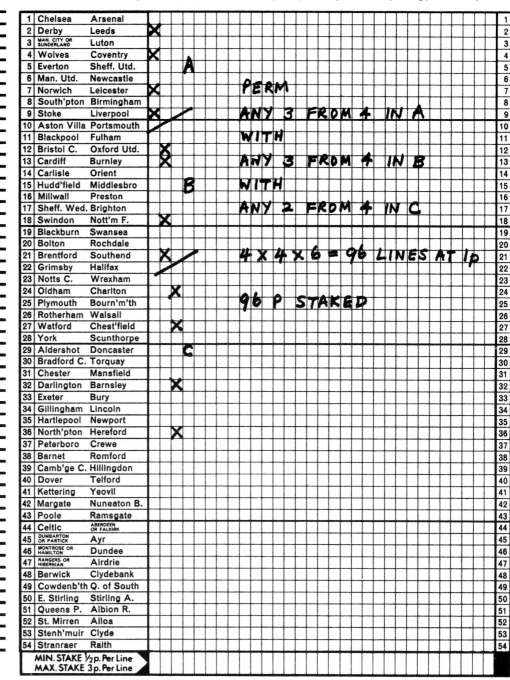

Diagram 9:4 Treble chance perms

war, the Treble Chance pool was invented. This was a master stroke and in 1950 Littlewoods paid the first £100,000 dividend. In 1972 a Mr Grimes won £512,683 and shortly afterwards the total payout in one week exceeded £1 million. Over £100 million is now staked annually on the Littlewoods coupon alone.

With such sums involved, security is of paramount importance. Large security forces contain retired detectives and policemen. Sophisticated equipment times the arrival of coupons and records them on microfilm. The thousands of employees are helped by electronic reading and sorting machines and computers. After Saturday's matches 12,000,000

coupons are checked and the dividends calculated and published by the following Wednesday. Pools firms like to publicize big winners, but clients who put an X in the appropriate place on their coupon will find their anonymity respected. Bad publicity about foolish behaviour by winners unaccustomed to wealth led to Littlewoods setting up a Winners' Advisory Service, and the company is anxious to provide expert help on investments and the sensible use of the winnings.

Little of the pools firms' wealth is ploughed back into the game which supports this financial empire, and with many soccer clubs facing bankruptcy, lovers of the game are expressing concern and looking to the pools for salvation. Unfortunately, there seems little room for a further cut from the stake money to be diverted to the clubs. A flourishing 'Fixed Odds' betting business, where winning gamblers were paid a fixed amount (say 35–1 for three draws), was killed with the introduction of a 25 per cent government tax. Punters would not take kindly to another sum being deducted from their already poor pools returns.

Football-pool gamblers use skill in forecasting, but in the Treble Chance pool those using skill are joined by millions backing lucky numbers or birthday-dates or other private systems. Those trusting to luck are not at a great disadvantage, as draws are the most difficult results to forecast. The pools represent an optimistic flutter rather than a serious gamble: the percentage disadvantage to the real gambler is too high.

However, there is one weakness in the Littlewoods Rules which a gambler can operate to his advantage. So far as the author is aware this has never before been pointed out in print. Rule 10, section c, subsection (i) of the Rules for 1972–73 states that bettors on the Four Draws pool will be paid one-half of the declared dividend if their forecast includes one void match with three correct.

Now, the odds against forecasting a draw can hardly ever be less than 3–1, so it would be more realistic to pay a bettor with 3 draws and a void only one quarter of the full dividend. Since odd matches are frequently postponed or rearranged after the coupon has been printed, it is possible for a gambler deliberately to include a void match in his Four Draws entry, and thus convert the pool, so far as he is concerned, into a Three Draws pool at comparatively favourable odds.

... and what happens to them when they win.
A happy pools winner after the presentation, with
the story in one hand and the champagne in the
other

With the deductions from the pool, can the
gambler be sure that the 'comparatively favourable'
odds have passed the point where they are
positively to his advantage?

Suppose there are 53 matches on the coupon, and
one is known in advance to be void. Suppose every
combination of four draws from the remaining 52
matches is backed equally by pools clients. There are
270,725 such combinations, and if each carried a
combined stake of £1, the pool would be £270,725.
Suppose half of this is deducted for tax, etc., the
payout to winners would be £135,362. Suppose
there were eight draws in those 52 matches. There
are 70 combinations of four from eight, so there will
be £70 staked on winning lines: the declared
dividend would be approximately £193 to 10p.

Suppose a gambler made the void match a banker
on the Four Draws and combined with it any 3 of
the remaining 52 matches. It would take 22,100 lines
and cost him a stake of £2,210 at 10p a line. He

would win 56 half-dividends (any 3 from 8 = 56).
His dividends would total £5,404, a profit of £3,194.

Does this work in practice? On February 24, 1973,
there were two void matches in the Littlewoods list
of 53. In the other 51 matches there were 12 draws.
The dividend was £75.75 for 10p. Had a gambler
taken one of the void matches as a banker and combined it with any three of the 51 matches that were
played, the bet would have cost him £2,082.50 at
10p stakes. He would have won 220 half-dividends,
or £8,332.50. A profit of £6,250, or almost exactly
300 per cent, in one afternoon without the need
to make a single forecast!

Profits would have been made on whichever
coupon was chosen from the Pools Promotors
Association's members, and indeed on two of the
pools the profit would have been greater. Dividends,
of course, vary with the number and popularity of
the draws which occur, and dividends in the week
mentioned were exceptionally high considering
there were 12 draws. The system will not necessarily
make a profit every time it is used. However, the
rule which allows such a bet is a bad one, and it has
been shown that smart gamblers can use it to
very considerable advantage. Of course, after the
publication of this book, it could well be changed.

# Famous GAMBLERS BETS & FRAUDS

## Chapter 10

Most men who make a living from gambling are either proprietors, like bookmakers or casino owners, or the people who work for them, like croupiers or clerks. The professional punter exists, but he is rare. An early example was Casanova, the great lover, who earned a living from gambling in the eighteenth century, although since if he lost his capital, there was no shortage of mistresses willing to replace it, it is not known if he was genuinely successful. His fame doesn't rest on gambling, of course, and neither does that of Sean Connery, whose nerve and luck, if not his skill, were proved at the St Vincent casino in 1963 when he backed No. 17 to win three times running at roulette, and it did. The odds against are 50,651–1, and Connery won about £10,000. It could almost have been a scene from one of his James Bond films.

Many Hollywood stars are devotees of horse-racing, which is popular in California. Bing Crosby has some good horses in his stable and in 1934 was a founder of the Santa Anita race-track near Hollywood, one of the biggest tracks in America, and was also president of the Del Mar track near Los Angeles.

British kings and queens have been keen patrons of racing. Lord Derby and Lord Rosebery are names famous on the Turf. The spiritual leader of the Ismaili community, the late Aga Khan, had the very best stables, and won the Derby five times. He was also a regular figure at the casinos of France and Monte Carlo.

None of these owners bet like Bernard Sunley, however. He was owner of the 1964 Derby runner Santa Claus and bet £6,000 each way on the horse at odds of 9¼–1. Santa Claus won (at a starting price of 15–8) and Ladbrokes, the bookmakers, claimed that the winnings of £69,375 was the biggest payout ever made by a bookmaker to one client on a single winner. Sunley also staked £20,000 to win £100,000 on his horse Out and About in the Mildmay of Flete Challenge Cup at Cheltenham the same year, but this time his horse was unplaced.

In 1924, Arnold Rothstein, an American racketeer, owned a racehorse called Sidereal. Convinced that it would win a particular race, Rothstein formed a syndicate of wealthy friends to back Sidereal with various bookmakers, the wagers to be placed at the last minute to avoid upsetting the odds. When Sidereal won at 40–1, the syndicate collected nearly $800,000.

Arnold Rothstein was famous as the man who 'fixed' the World's Series in 1919. He appears as Meyer Wolfshein in Scott Fitzgerald's novel The *Great Gatsby*. It was alleged (but never proved, despite confessions by some of the players) that Rothstein paid $100,000 to Chicago White Sox baseball players to lose a match with Cincinnatti. Rothstein won $350,000, betting on Cincinnatti. Rothstein and the Chicago White Sox players were brought to trial: Rothstein managed to be acquitted. He was not so lucky with the law of the underworld, however. After refusing to pay huge losses incurred at poker he was shot in the stomach and killed in 1928.

In the nineteenth century, John Gully and William Crockford were rival bookmakers. Gully's career was as remarkable as Crockford's. He was put into Fleet Prison for not paying a debt, but bought out again by Henry Pearce, prize-fighting champion of England, who noticed Gully's fine physique and saw in him a worthy crowd-pulling opponent. Gully became champion himself. In later years, as well as being a bookmaker, he owned a coal-mine and was

Casanova, as portrayed in a 1970 Health Education Council leaflet advocating birth control, in which field Casanova was a non-gambler

M.P. for Pontefract. William Crockford owned Sultan in the Derby of 1819, and he backed the horse heavily with Gully, who was convinced Tiresias would win. In the event Tiresias beat Sultan by half a neck. Just before the St Leger Sultan broke down. Gully heard of the mishap first and managed to take Crockford's bets before Crockford himself heard the news. Hatred reigned. In 1827, Gully secretly bought the Derby winner, Mameluke. He was thought to be a 'clever' Derby winner, having just beaten his stable companion Glenartney whom many suspected to be the better horse. Gully backed Mameluke with Crockford to win £45,000 on the St Leger, and then revealed his ownership. Crockford was furious. Mameluke was an excitable horse, and there was all sorts of bother at the start of the St Leger, calculated to work him into a lather. When the field got away at about the eighth attempt, Mameluke was left by several yards. He fought his way through in a rough race, but was finally beaten by a length. The starter was later dismissed. Gully lost his money to Crockford, and who knows how much of it was forwarded to the starter and the other jockeys for a job well done?

A more recent example of bookmaker biting bookmaker occurred in the 1950s, although no shady business was involved. The firm of William Hill specialized in asking punters, through newspaper advertisements, to name the first four in certain races, and paid out to the few lucky winners a handsome dividend, calculated by multiplying the odds. The firm of Shermans decided to run a similar advertisement. Calling hundreds of employees together, Hills gave them £1 each and asked them to back the same horses to finish in the same order. Of course, had the result been correct, Shermans would have faced a mammoth payout, so they had to cancel the bets, place an ignominious notice to this effect in *The Sporting Life* and return all stakes.

Gully and Crockford featured in the 1844 Derby scandal, the most notorious case of a 'ringer'. They owned the two favourites, and while public form suggested that Crockford's horse, Ratan, was the better, Gully persisted in backing his horse, The Ugly Buck. It seemed evil work might be afoot, particularly when it was discovered that the son of Crockford's trainer had also backed The Ugly Buck with Gully. In the event, Ratan was found to be doped, but both Crockford and Gully were out-swindled by an audacious trickster called Goodman Levy, or Abraham Levi Goodman. Levy owned a 2-year-old called Running Rein and a 3-year-old called Maccabeus. By constantly switching their stables he managed to confuse their identities. When Running Rein won a 2-year-old race in 1843, after Levy had backed him from 10–1 to 3–1, many judges thought him to be the best-developed 2-year-old they'd ever seen, and the Duke of Rutland, who owned the second horse, objected to him. It could not be proved that the horse was not Running Rein, and Levy collected his money. Lord George Bentinck was convinced that Running Rein was really Maccabeus, and during the winter he collected evidence to support his view. Five days before the Derby, he asked the Stewards to inquire into the identity of Running Rein, but his request was refused. Levy, meanwhile, had given Running Rein to Alexander Wood of Epsom in payment for corn. Wood was an innocent dupe in the swindle. Running Rein ran in his name in the Derby and Levy backed it to win £50,000. Running Rein won. There was pandemonium. Bookmakers refused to pay; instead of leading in his winner Mr Wood went home to bed; Colonel Peel, the owner of the second horse, objected; and the Stewards withheld the stakes pending an inquiry.

Colonel Peel, a brother of Prime Minister Sir Robert, was not anxious to be party to a scandal, but those staunch upholders of turf honour, Lord George Bentinck and Admiral Rous, persuaded him to take the case to law. Wood was forced to sue the Jockey Club to get his stake money; Colonel Peel was the defendant as Jockey Club representative. The defence was that Running Rein was really the ineligible 4-year-old Maccabeus, and in fact Lord George Bentinck had discovered a shopkeeper who had sold Levy large quantities of dye. The judge, of course, asked for Running Rein to be produced. When it was known that Levy had removed Running Rein from Wood the day before and that both had disappeared, the case was virtually settled. Colonel Peel's Orlando was declared the winner of the 1844 Derby: Levy died in poverty in France.

This was not the end of the 1844 Derby story. It was also suspected that two shady German brothers called Lichtwald were running 4-year-olds, called Leander and Julia, in the Derby and Oaks. Neither won, and Leander fell and was destroyed. When he was exhumed, his lower jaw was mysteriously missing! Experts claimed, however, that the upper jaw was that of a 4-year-old and the Lichtwald brothers were disqualified for ever from the British Turf. They said afterwards, from the safety of Germany, that the horse was in fact 6.

A sad postscript to all this is the story of Sir Victor Sassoon's crack horse Pinturischio, in 1961. Because of a temperature, he missed the Dante Stakes at York, and was afterwards suspected of being doped. He was found to be poisoned before the Derby, for which he had for a long time been the favourite, and he never ran again.

Colourful characters like Gully, Crockford and Lord George Bentinck are not to be found on the Turf these days. Perhaps the last great gambler was Bob Sievier, who died in 1939. He owned the peerless filly Sceptre, one of only two ever to have won four Classic races. He himself won and lost several fortunes. He went to the Epsom spring meeting in 1888 with £25, and left three days later with £16,000. In 1900 he won over £60,000 at four meetings, £33,000 coming from the victory of Grafter in the City and Suburban. These were large sums in those days. He was several times before the Courts, and was nearly broken when losing a libel action against Richard Wootton; he was warned off the Turf. In another celebrated court case, he won a popular and spectacular victory when charged with blackmailing Jack Joel. He was generous, and died a poor man, but his 79 years could hardly have been packed with more rumbustious incident.

Sean Connery at the roulette table at St Vincent where he won £10,000. Note the stake on 17

An American counterpart to Sievier was John 'Bet-A-Million' Gates. Gates made money with a barbed-wire factory, was head of a steel corporation, plunged successfully in Wall Street, and became a multi-millionaire. He was a shrewd operator who would bet on anything – provided he thought the odds were in his favour. It is said that he once won $20,000 on a train journey betting on raindrops running down a window pane. He also lost a quarter of a million dollars in one day on the racecourse. He was given his nickname of 'Bet-A-Million' after a race-track official had asked him to limit his bets to $10,000. Insulted, he immediately offered to bet a million dollars on a horse if anybody would take the bet. Nobody did.

If the big racing gamblers are flamboyant, the best card players are shrewd and analytical. Ely Culbertson, the master bridge player, would not only bet heavily on his matches, he would increase the bets when losing, no doubt in an attempt to achieve psychological supremacy over his opponents.

The greatest casino card player was Nico Zographos, the head of the Greek Syndicate. The other three original members of the syndicate were

Eli Eliopulo, Zaret Couyoumdjian and Athanase Vagliano. At baccarat, the bank is auctioned among the players. The highest bidder takes the bank, and his bid is the amount he must put up for the other players to bet against. In 1922 at Deauville, Nico Zographos announced '*Tout va*', meaning that there was no limit; he was prepared to cover any bet that anybody wanted to make. He thus pitted the entire wealth of the Syndicate against the world's best and biggest gamblers.

Zographos was an intellectual, the son of a Greek professor of Political Economy. His card counting was superb. At baccarat six packs (312 cards) are dealt from a shoe until less than nine cards remain, when six new packs are shuffled, cut and placed in the shoe. It was said that when the nine cards were left at the end Zographos could more often than not name them.

The Syndicate took on the world's most famous gamblers, winning and losing huge amounts, sometimes being nearly broke, at other times being

The late Aga Khan leads in Blenheim, the 1930 Derby winner, Harry Wragg up. The famous tipster Prince Monolulu is behind.

millionaires. In later years they played for the casinos. Over £1,000 million passed through Zographos's hands in his career. When he died in 1953 he left over £5 million.

Gordon Selfridge, founder of the famous London store, was a victim of the Syndicate. He haunted the casinos in the 1920s, usually with the Dolly Sisters, a Hungarian cabaret act. Selfridge fell in love with one sister and sponsored the gambling of both. He was a big gambler himself, and in seven years lost about £2 million. He left only about £2,000 when he died, and owed Zographos £80,000.

Zographos also won a fortune from André Citroën, the French motor-car manufacturer. Citroën obtained so much publicity from losing heavily, he sometimes claimed it was worth losing. In 1926, he temporarily lost control of his factory after losing 13 million francs to Zographos in one session. Citroën's wife gatecrashed the baccarat room, where women were not allowed, and wept and pleaded with Zographos not to play any more. Zographos, who was always courteous and a good loser himself, closed the session. In the same years that Selfridge was losing his money, Citroën lost

Arnold Rothstein

Santa Claus, Scobie Breasley up, was the medium of a huge gamble by owner Bernard Sunley to win the 1964 Derby.

thirty million francs to Zographos, and eventually did lose his business altogether.

A rich American once offered to play Zographos one hand of baccarat for a million francs (about £60,000). Zographos suggested the best of three hands. The wager was made, Zographos lost the first hand, then won the next two and the bet.

The members of Greek Syndicate were honest, and their wins were based on skill. They made no more than 1 per cent profit on their turnover, and had their spectacular losses as well as wins. A Chilean finance minister once won 17 million francs from Zographos and offered to play 'double or quits'. For once in his life Zographos was forced to refuse a bet.

In 1928, Zographos lost heavily for a long time. He was, in fact, down to his last million francs, which formed what could have been the Syndicate's last bank. Knowing the situation, the big gamblers took up the challenge and the million francs were at stake on one coup. The players of the two hands against Zographos were satisfied with their cards. Zographos's two cards were the King of Hearts and Queen of Spades, worth exactly nothing. Amid great

Pinturischio, Lester Piggot up.

Above: John 'Bet-A-Million' Gates, rich American gambler
Below: Robert S. Sievier, owner, bookmaker and big punter

tension, the imperturbable Zographos drew his third card and impassively turned it over. It was the Nine of Diamonds, a legendary card known in other connections as the Pope and the Curse of Scotland, and it was the best Zographos could have drawn. He had won, and he made the Nine of Diamonds his personal emblem: it was on his crockery, his cuff-links, his yacht pennant. The Greek Syndicate was never again in danger. It still operates, with new members, some of them descendants of the old, and still wins more than it loses.

A notable coup at roulette was brought off by two students at Reno in 1947. Albert Hibbs and Roy Walford, who later became a space scientist and a professor of medicine respectively, logged a roulette wheel at the Palace Club, found a fault, and betting in half-dollars from a bank of $100 ran up winnings of $5,000 before the wheel was changed. They then repeated the operation at Harolds Club, were once $13,000 to the good, and finally left with a student's fortune of $7,000 and immense publicity.

It was said in the section on blackjack that, played properly, this game could provide a profit for gamblers. An American mathematics professor, Edward O. Thorpe, explained in a book, *Beat the Dealer,* published in 1962 and later revised, exactly how it was done. Unfortunately, to put Professor Thorpe's system into practice, or even to understand it, one needs almost to be a professor of mathematics oneself. Undoubtedly the system works, and Thorpe won much money with it before he was banned from casinos in Las Vegas.

America's most famous gambler is a man whose career is like that of Nico Zographos. He is Nicholas Dandolos, like Zographos an intellectual (he has a degree in philosophy) and also an expert card-player, although his favourite game is stud poker. He is known as Nick the Greek. He, too, always played honestly, and in his career had several million dollars pass through his hands. He knew extremes of poverty and wealth, and claimed to have slept less than any man who ever lived. Money meant little to Nick the Greek. He was very careless with it and cigars were his only luxury. He gambled for the joy of it, win or lose, often for days and nights at a stretch. He made Las Vegas the centre of his operations in the early days of the boom, and crowds would come to watch him make his huge bets in casinos.

A society scandal which rocked Victorian England in 1891 concerned the Prince of Wales and baccarat, which he enjoyed and introduced into England. He carried his own cards and counters with him (betting on cards was illegal in England at the time), and took them to a house party at Tranby Croft, where he was staying for the Doncaster St Leger race meeting of 1890. The party consisted of a number of lords and ladies, military men and society stalwarts. Sir William Gordon-Cumming, baronet, soldier, Scottish landowner and eligible bred-in-the-purple bachelor, was in the party at the Prince's invitation.

On the first night of baccarat, Stanley Wilson, the young son of the host, thought he detected Gordon-Cumming practising the sleight of hand

Gordon Selfridge, store tycoon and big spender in Continental casinos, at the 1929 Grand National

known as *la pousette*; in other words he was illegally and surreptitiously altering his stake once he knew the value of his hand. After the game, he communicated his suspicions to other shocked members of the party and on the second night Gordon-Cumming was closely watched. Another member of the party, Mr Edward Lycett Green, agreed with Stanley Wilson and eventually the Prince of Wales was informed of the situation by Lord Coventry and General Owen Williams. A committee decided that the scandal must be hushed up, and although strenuously denying his guilt, Gordon-Cumming was persuaded to sign a paper that he would never play cards again in return for silence by all parties. Next day he left the house. There the affair might have ended, but a few months later Gordon-Cumming received an anonymous note from Paris telling him that everybody was discussing the incident. To clear his name, Gordon-Cumming then sought retractions from the people who claimed to have seen him cheat. These were not forthcoming, and Gordon-Cumming sued for slander. The Prince of Wales was called to give evidence.

The case was evenly fought, and all England now knew that the Prince of Wales spent his evenings gambling. The knowledge pained Queen Victoria. Gordon-Cumming was splendid in the witness box, while some of the five defendants were a little shaky. However weight of numbers told and the jury acquitted. Gordon-Cumming was ostracized. The Prince admitted an error of judgment in attempting to conceal the incident, and Queen Victoria had some words to say about his alarming and shocking habits. Later Gordon-Cumming's wife expressed the opinion that her husband had been framed for having crossed the Prince in an affair of the heart, and there were others who agreed that the evidence against him was some way short of convincing.

A delightful racing swindle which worked occurred in England in 1880. The Editor of *Bell's Life*, now amalgamated with *The Sporting Life*, received a letter from the Secretary of the Trodmore Hunt asking him to publish the enclosed Easter Monday racing programme and promising to send the results by telegram. Easter is a busy time for racing men, with upwards of a dozen meetings taking place, and the Editor was glad of this assistance and duly published. The results arrived, and were also published the following day. Several illegal

Motor car manufacturer and big loser
André Citroën

betting-shop proprietors in London paid out several thousand pounds to lucky backers. There was then a query about the starting price of a horse, another paper having printed 7–2 where *Bell's* had 5–2, and the Trodmore Hunt had to be contacted to resolve it. Of course, no such place as Trodmore exists.

Another neat and successful coup also depended upon the heavy Bank Holiday racing programme and it was pulled off as recently as 1953 at Huntingdon. The official starting price of racehorses is decided by a group of racing journalists who note the prices on offer at the time of the 'off'. They are dedicated men, and normally no queries or complaints arise from either bookmakers or punters. On this occasion a horse called C.D.B. won, and he could be backed on the course at prices around 7–4. Because there were about 16 race meetings, the starting-price journalists were thin on the ground, and a reporter pressed into service was convinced by a group of bookmakers that they were offering 25–1. That became the official starting price. Off-course bookmakers could do nothing about it and were forced to pay out £200,000.

Another coup attempted in 1953 did not work. A French horse called Santa Amaro ran in the 2 o'clock race at Bath on July 16 in the name of an inferior French horse called Francascal. It won at 10–1. The horse had been backed with bookmakers in London to win over £50,000. The reason the horse started at such good odds was that the telephone lines to Bath were not open, and the blower service was unable to transfer this money to the course. Had the bookmakers with the liabilities been able to phone their commissions through, Francascal would have started at considerably shorter odds, perhaps only 2–1 instead of 10–1. A road-sweeper was instrumental in uncovering the plot when he reported having seen two men with a ladder and what looked like a post-office van in a quiet lane near Bath. The police decided that the line had been deliberately cut, and apprehended a man who had been paid to cut it. Four men were eventually sentenced for organizing the crime. The investigations revealed the 'ringer'; and both Francascal and Santa Amaro were barred from racing for ever. One member of the gang, a Welsh bookmaker, was shot dead on his doorstep some years later by men looking for money he was popularly believed to have stacked away inside.

The plot failed because the gang was too greedy. Had it been content with just the switching of the horses, and smaller profits, the coup would have resembled many others 'legitimately' brought off, and bookmakers would have been rueful, but not unduly suspicious. The mistake was the cutting of the telephone wire.

Would the operation have been successful otherwise? It is quite likely. The bookmakers, had the blower service been available, would have shared a loss of a few thousand pounds, but cannot cause a furore every time a successful gamble is landed. This raises the question of whether or not less spectacular and better planned swindles have escaped detection. While racing men can congratulate themselves on the apparent comparative lack of racecourse crime, they cannot afford complacency.

Greed led to the failure of the biggest coup of all in 1964. It was allied to a contempt for appearances which led the instigators to make no effort to disguise the swindle. Had the crooks been successful, they would have netted about £10 million from Britain's bookmakers. Anybody who expects to part bookmakers and this sort of money is a dreamer! The scene was Dagenham greyhound stadium on the afternoon of June 30, 1964, and betting was taking place on the 4·05 race. The only people betting at the forecast windows were a gang of hefty men equipped with bags of silver who were dissuading with very unsubtle strong-arm methods any other members of the public from placing a bet. By the time the race was run they had bought a few hundred forecast tickets, but only one ticket correctly placed the two dogs which finished first and second. This ticket scooped the pool, and the dividend declared was an unheard-of £987. 11s. 6d. for 2s., colossal odds of nearly 10,000–1. Of course the gang were not after the tote return on the track, which merely repaid them their stakes, less commission. All over the country accomplices had been backing the winning forecast in betting shops and with bookmakers in small amounts totalling around £1,000. They had even taken the precaution of jamming telephone lines to the stadium.

It seems unlikely that the gang could have so

misjudged the size of the dividend or the gullibility of bookmakers to expect to escape suspicion. More likely they were prepared to brazen it out, since the dividend was officially declared and they held legitimate winning vouchers from bookmakers. Naturally bookmakers fell back on the tactic of withholding payment while inquiries were made, and most followed the final Victoria Club decision to declare the race void and return all winning and losing stakes. Some obviously genuine backers were paid out on a calculation of what a fair tote return might have been. The gang could hardly go to law, although a few individual actions were fought.

As with the Francascal case, the gang might have been successful had they not been so thorough.

The Prince of Wales (with cap) in 1899. He owned great race-horses and was a keen card player, introducing baccarat to England

A more gentle manipulation of the tote return could have been achieved without monopolizing the windows and a respectable profit could have been made.

And it is not enough for bookmakers and the Greyhound Racing Association to be satisfied that the coup failed. After all, the gang bought hundreds of tickets on combinations that didn't win, and only one ticket on the correct forecast. There must have been some meddling with the greyhounds themselves.

113

# LOTTERIES
## and other gambles

Lotteries are gambles in which the participants buy numbered tickets. Winning numbers are determined by a method involving chance, and prizes distributed to the holders of the corresponding tickets. Simple raffles are the commonest form. They are popular as fund-raisers with charities and sports clubs, the prizes usually donated by well-wishers. For ticket-buyers they are a painless way of supporting good causes.

Although governments throughout the world find lotteries an acceptable method of raising revenue, the only national lottery run in Britain is the Premium Bonds scheme. Bonds can be bought at most Post Offices, banks and Trustee Savings Banks, in blocks of various denominations, and can be cashed at their face value at any time, but no interest is paid on them, the hypothetical interest forming the pool from which winners are paid. Electronic Random Number Indicator Equipment – ERNIE – generates the winning numbers. The unit is £1 and there are monthly and weekly draws, prizes ranging from £50,000 to £25.

A lottery which has flourished since the 1930s, despite the fact that it is illegal everywhere except Ireland, is the Irish Hospitals' Sweepstake. A Dublin company, Hospital Trust (1940) Limited, is authorized by the government to run the sweep for the benefit of Irish hospitals. Tickets for the sweep are sold by agents who smuggle them into countries all over the world: Great Britain, the United States and Canada are the biggest markets. The sweep is based on a few major horse races a year: currently the Lincolnshire and Cambridgeshire Handicaps, the Irish Derby and the Irish Sweeps Hurdle. Millions of tickets at £1 are sold on each race. The stubs are returned to Dublin, where at a grand ceremony the names of the runners and the ticket numbers are drawn from separate drums by Irish nurses, while the Irish police maintain security. Any ticket-holder who draws a horse is guaranteed £400. Large prizes are paid to the drawers of the horses which finish in the first three: the payout on the winning horse might be over £100,000. Because of its illegality abroad, requiring the employment of thousands of 'secret' agents, the expenses of running the sweep are high, and early in 1973 newspapers asked questions about the percentage of receipts finding its way to the hospitals.

Bingo is a lottery. It is very popular in America, and since the 1960s has enjoyed a boom in Britain, where the decline of filmgoing led to many cinemas being converted into bingo halls. Players buy cards (the purchase price is their stake) on which are squares numbered with 24 of the numbers between 1 and 90 (1–75 is the range in America). Each card

bears a different combination of numbers. Table tennis balls numbered 1–90 are ejected from a cage and the numbers announced by a caller. When a number is called, players with that number on their card cancel it. When a player has all his numbers cancelled, he shouts 'Bingo', and after his card has been checked he wins the prize. Sometimes prizes are awarded to the first player with a line or column filled rather than the whole card. This sort of high-speed bingo was noted in 1973 by the British Gaming Board, who were concerned that excessive action might creep into the neighbourhood game. The majority of bingo players come from low-income groups and over 80 per cent are women. A typical

Above: The ERNIE control desk, with the officer responsible for the prize draw
Below: A premium bond

Above: the draw for the Irish Hospitals'
Sweepstake in the Plaza Ballroom, Dublin.
Below: Bingo at a Granada club

bingo addict has been defined: a working-class wife spending most of her free time in the bingo palaces. With the players sitting sedately in rows, studying their cards, bingo is hardly exciting, and perhaps the majority of players are attracted as much by the refreshment breaks and the companionship as by the gambling element.

The American policy or numbers game has a turnover greater even than bingo. Basically, the gambler bets on a 3-digit number between 000 and 999. He makes his bet with an agent of a 'numbers' bank. Although the game is illegal, most Americans know who their local agents are. Bets are made by writing a number and stake on a pad, e.g. 827 – $1. Two carbons are made: the bettor has one slip, the agent a second and the third is forwarded by runner to the bank. A winning number is announced, winners are paid, and a new numbers game starts. That is the game reduced to its essentials. Different methods have been used to determine the winning number. In the late 1920s, when the game began to be popular, the last three figures of the daily Federal Reserve Clearing House report were used. This allowed a daily game and eliminated cheating, as these numbers could not be manipulated and were published in the newspapers. Nowadays the official payoff prices at a pre-selected race-track are often used to determine winners. The odds paid to bettors on the correct number vary according to the bank: it might be 550–1, from which 10 per cent will be deducted for the runner's commission, so the winner will get back about half what he would expect were he paid out at the true odds. All numbers have a 999–1 chance of winning, but some numbers (like 777 for instance) are far more popular with backers than others. To insure against heavy losses, banks will pay shorter odds on these numbers. They are called 'cut numbers', and the bank may pay only 400–1 on them. Some banks might list 200 or so cut numbers, thus increasing their own profits nicely. Bets other than those on straight numbers are possible, and are invented and discarded as the bank finds it necessary to inspire business. An example is the box number. A box drawn around the number 345, say, will win if the winning number is any combination of those three digits: 345, 354, 435, 453, 534, 543. It is really a bet on six numbers, and the odds will be $\frac{1}{6}$ of those paid on a single number: 100–1 or just below.

In the 1930s the numbers game was taken over and organized by gangsters, who did not always bother to pay winners: it became popularly known as the 'numbers racket'. Dutch Schultz, a New York mobster, was an early numbers-racket king, but like one or two others in this book he was soon shot dead by an unknown ill-wisher.

Keno is a lottery found in many American casinos and carnivals. An electric scoreboard contains the numbers 1–80. At specified times 20 winning numbers are selected by means of table tennis balls drawn from a cage and the numbers are lit up on the scoreboard. Between times a player can back numbers of his choice. There are various combinations possible: he can back one number, two numbers or groups of numbers up to 15. By far the most popular bet, which accounts for 80 per cent of the business, is a group of ten numbers, known as the 10-spot ticket. If all ten of the player's numbers appear in the winning 20, he will be paid out the apparently splendid odds of 25,000 for 1. Nor does it end there: if he has nine numbers right he will get 2,800 for 1; eight numbers right pays 1,400; seven numbers 180; six numbers 18 and five numbers 2. If four or fewer numbers are correct, the ticket is a loser. To put these odds into perspective, it can be calculated that the chance of all ten of a player's numbers appearing in the 20 chosen out of 80 is one in about 9,000,000. The player on the 10-spot ticket will collect about once in 15 times, and over 80 per cent of these wins will be for picking five numbers, where the win will be of one unit only.

A player betting on just one number will be paid $3·20 for a $1 ticket if that number is among the 20: odds of 2·2–1. The correct odds are 3–1, and the bank's advantage is 20 per cent. The bank's advantage on all the Keno bets varies little from 20 per cent, so it is an unattractive game from the punter's point of view.

Slot machines can be likened to lotteries. The player puts a coin into a slot and pulls a handle which spins three wheels, each containing 20 symbols (not all different: some symbols appear a few times on each wheel and there may be only six

Above: Big Bertha and shapely gambler, Las Vegas
Below: Lucky Strike and English misses, Henley Royal Regatta, 1971

*different* symbols in all). When the wheels stop, three symbols, one on each wheel, are showing, and the machine is made so that certain combinations, usually about ten, will pay off a certain number of coins. The symbols used are usually fruit: cherries, plums, oranges, etc. If there were only one cherry on each wheel, the chance of getting the three cherries in the line showing would be one in $20 \times 20 \times 20$, or one in 8,000. This might be the jackpot line, paying, say, 200 coins. It might be that another winning line is three oranges. For ease of reckoning, let us assume there are four oranges on each wheel, i.e. it is 4–1 against an orange showing

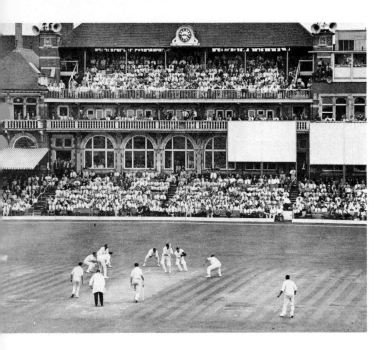

Betting takes place on cricket (above: England v Australia, The Oval) and golf (below: Gary Player and Jack Nicklaus)

and on the punter's side cunning methods of cheating have been devised, but modern technology has foiled the latter, and the former is really unnecessary, since a legitimate percentage can be guaranteed. Slot machines are usually known in Britain as fruit machines, because of the symbols; in America one-armed bandits is the popular term, because of the one handle or arm, and the tendency to 'rob' punters of their coins.

Most sports provide means for betting, even cricket, that gentle pastime of languorous summers. At many big matches in England since 1970 a discreet bookmaker's office has quoted odds during play on batsmen scoring centuries, or on the time of the winning hit or anything else suitable. Betting on golf is big business at American tournaments, and in 1972 a betting marquee appeared for the first time on a British course, at Turnberry. The bookmakers were delighted with the spectators' response, but the golfing establishment views betting with wariness.

A method for betting on American football and basketball has been devised by American bookmakers. The bookmaker estimates the likely difference in points between the two sides; this is then added to the weaker team's actual score for the purposes of betting. For instance the bookmaker might quote Team A a 10-point favourite over Team B. This means that bettors on Team A win if their team wins by more than 10 points; bettors on Team B win if their team is beaten by fewer than 10 points. If the difference is exactly 10 points, the bet is off. Bookmakers will take bets on either team, but both teams will be odds-on, either 6–5 or 11–10 according to the bookmaker and the standing of the client. Doubles and trebles are accepted and known as 'parlays'. A bookmaker offering odds of 5–6 for the single will offer 12–5 for a two-team parlay and 5–1 for a three-team parlay.

Baseball bets are made in more conventional fashion with odds quoted about each team. The odds might be quoted thus: '1·80–1·40 Yankees favourites'. This means that bettors on Yankees must lay 180 units to win 100; backers of the opponents will win 140 units for 100. On this example the advantage to the bookmaker is nearly 6 per cent. The same odds might be quoted by some bookmakers as '9–7 Yankees favourites', meaning the Yankees are 9–5 on, and the opposition 7–5 against.

Boxing has always been popular with gamblers, perhaps because it is such a physical sport. Repressed aggressive instincts might lead some people to find both boxing and gambling attractive. Because there has always been a feeling that fights are frequently crooked or fixed, bookmakers are not over-anxious to bet on them, and when they do they usually want a good percentage. Most betting is therefore private. In the days of prize fighting, champions were sponsored by the aristocracy and betting was high. In the eighteenth century, the Duke of Cumberland sponsored John Broughton, who has a commemorative stone in Westminster Abbey, and lost £50,000 when Broughton was beaten in his last fight. When Jack Dempsey fought

on any one wheel. The chance of three oranges would be one in 5 × 5 × 5, or one in 125; the line might pay off 10 coins. If another winning line on this slot machine were cherry–cherry–orange the chance of getting it would be one in 20 × 20 × 5, or one in 2,000; the payoff might again be 10 coins. The winning lines are decided arbitrarily. So are the payoffs, and they may bear no relation to the probability of the lines. Unless one knows how many of each symbol are on each wheel, it is impossible to calculate the percentage profit the slot machine will make: obviously machines can be manufactured to make the percentage profit required. Slot machines are big business in Nevada, where they can be found in some casinos in rows of hundreds. In Great Britain they are usually found singly in clubs and public houses. Crooked machines have been made,

Jess Willard for the world championship in 1919, he bet his purse of $10,000 at odds of 10–1 that he would beat Willard in the first round. Willard was down seven times in the opening round and took the full count. Dempsey left the ring, but his joy at winning $100,000 was short-lived: the timekeeper pointed out that when a new ring canvas had been laid the bell had been muted, and that 'time' had saved Willard. Dempsey returned to knock out Willard in the third round and win the title, but he had lost his $100,000 bet. World-title fights are the biggest attractions for gamblers. There are often shocks, and George Foreman was a 5–2 underdog when knocking out Joe Frazier for the heavyweight championship in 1973.

Hardly a sport escapes its gamblers. There have been attempts to bet on motor racing, usually unsuccessful. Although the authorities at the Wimbledon tennis championships, with their strawberries-and-cream traditions, will not allow betting, this does not prevent bookmakers publishing lists of odds in newspapers.

Greyhound racing is a sport which depends almost entirely on gambling. It is popular, though declining, in Britain. Its image is very different to that of horse-racing: it is a cloth-capped version of the sport of kings. There are usually eight races at a meeting, with six dogs running in each. The dogs

Americans bet on American football (above: Phantoms v Chicks) and baseball (below: Washington Senators v Oakland Athletics)

start in traps, each dog wearing a vest showing its trap colour and number. An electric hare circles the track on a rail, and as it passes the traps the doors fly open and the dogs chase the hare to the winning post. Few dogs inspire affection like great race-horses do, many bettors in fact not even bothering with their names but backing their trap numbers. Betting is through bookmakers or the track's tote, and dogs are backed to win or be placed, i.e. to be first or second. The tote runs a forecast pool on each race, where punters are required to pick the first two dogs in the correct order. Tote betting is based on trap numbers, not the greyhounds' names.

Betting on national and local elections has recently caught on in Britain, and the bookmaking firm of Ladbrokes, who did much pioneering work in election betting, took £1,600,000 in bets on the 1966 General Election. Most bets are on the size of the eventual majority. Betting on elections is popular in America, where one gambler is believed to have lost a million dollars when Kennedy defeated Nixon for

Below: Afternoon greyhound racing at New Cross.
Right: Betting on the 'Escape Stakes' in 1966, when British prisons had a spate of breakouts.
Opposite: Election betting, on the size of the majority at a British General Election, and on the election of an Italian President

the U.S. Presidency.

In Italy betting on the election of a new pope attracts a lot of business. Papal form is evidently reliable, as Cardinal Montini was favourite before his election in 1963. Britons are not to be outdone in betting on their superiors: many wagers were struck on the names the Queen would choose for her younger children.

A gamble which is found around racecourses and in side streets is the Three-card Trick, also known as the Three-card Monte and Find the Lady. It is not really a gamble at all but a swindle, and is illegal everywhere. An operator shows three cards, one of which is usually a Queen (hence 'Find the Lady'), deals them face down in a line onto a makeshift table, perhaps a suitcase, and moves them around. The punter has to watch closely and bet on where he thinks the Queen has been placed. He thinks he has merely to watch the rapid moving around of the cards, but in fact there are several tricks, including palming, which the operator uses to ensure the mug doesn't win. Sometimes the Queen appears to be marked with a bent corner, but when the mug pounces he finds another card has just acquired a bent corner. In fact, the Three-card Trick is operated by a mob. One at least will be a look-out. Two or three may be accomplices, allowed to 'win' in order to lure the mugs on. There is often a 'dip', or pickpocket, in the gang, whose job it is to remove wallets while everybody is watching the action. When the gang have made a sufficient killing, the look-out will pretend to spot the law, and the gang will melt away to meet later at a rendezvous to divide the spoils. Properly executed, it is a very

slick operation indeed.

Chuck-a-Luck is a dice game found in casinos, most often in America. The game is really the same as Crown and Anchor, described fully in Chapter Two. The difference is that conventional dice are used. They tumble around in a cage shaped like an hour-glass; when the cage is inverted the dice fall through the narrow opening. The betting board is divided into six parts, numbered 1–6. The payoffs, and the percentage disadvantage to the punter, are as listed for Crown and Anchor.

Fairs and carnivals provide numerous gambling

Above: Jack Dempsey (white shorts) punishes
Jess Willard in the first round of their world title
fight, 1919
Right: Illegal crap games in Cardiff's Tiger Bay
in 1953
Below: A Crown and Anchor gambling wheel in
Toronto

games. In some, the operator's advantage cannot be calculated. For instance, the game where coins are rolled onto numbered squares to win a payoff if they land in a square and to lose if they land on a line cannot be evaluated without knowing the diameter of the coins and the widths of the squares and lines. The game where balls are rolled through numbered arches is easier to assess, but in neither case will the calculation help the punter, unless it persuades him to give the stalls a wide berth.

Percentages can be calculated on such games as the Money Wheel, found in American casinos and carnivals. On a typical Money Wheel there might be fifty compartments, 22 of which contain a $1 bill, 14 a $2 bill, seven a $5 bill, three a $10 bill, two a $20 bill, one a flag and one a joker. The wheel is spun, and the winning compartment is that opposite an indicator when the wheel stops spinning. There are seven spaces on the betting layout, and the bettor can bet on any denomination from $1 to joker to win with $1 bills. If successful, he wins the value of the winning bill. The flag and joker pay 40–1. It is a simple calculation to work out the wheel's advantage on any bet: for instance, a bet on the $20 bills pays 20–1 but the correct odds are 24–1. Overall, the wheel enjoys an advantage of about 20 per cent.

In British fairs, a popular game is that in which a giant turntable is spun while on an electric indicator board the names of towns, or jockeys, are lit up in rotation. When the turntable stops, the winning town remains lit. The prize is a pick of the articles on display rather than a cash prize. If there are 60 towns on the board, the odds against winning are 59–1. The punter must decide whether the prize he has in mind is worth 60 times the cost of the ticket.

An ancient Oriental gambling game is Fan Tan. A handful of beans is placed under a bowl. Gamblers back one of the numbers 1–4. The bowl is then removed, and the beans are taken away four at a time. At the end, either 1,2,3 or 4 beans will remain, and the lucky punter will collect. The game is played privately. If the players take turns of the bank, they must pay 3–1 to winners for the game to be fair.

This game is not to be confused with the ancient game in which a known number of coins, pebbles or matches is placed in a pile, and two contestants take turns to draw 1,2 or 3 from it, the player forced to take the last being the loser. Simple arithmetic can win this game. All that is necessary is to ensure that the pile one's opponent draws from is always a number divisible by four, plus one, for instance 5,9,13,17, etc. When he is eventually left with five, no matter how many he draws, he can be forced to take the last one.

# Index

Numbers in italics refer to illustrations

# Acknowledgments  Bibliography

*The publishers are grateful to the following organisations for the illustrations in this book:*

Associated Press

Barnaby's Picture Library

P. Bertrand

Camera Press

Central Press Photos

Conway Picture Library

Joe Coral Ltd.

Daily Telegraph

Department of National Savings

Fox Photos

Freelance Photographers Guild

Granada Theatres Ltd.

Hamlyn Group Library

Horserace Totalisator Board

Keystone Press Agency

Littlewoods Pools

The Mansell Collection

Mary Evans Picture Library

National Film Archive

Paul Popper

Pictorial Press

Press Association

Syndication International

United Press International

**Beat the Dealer** by Edward O. Thorp. Blaisdell Publishing Co., New York, 1962. *A winning strategy for the game of 21.*

**The Big Wheel** by George W. Herald and Edward D. Radin. William Morrow and Co., New York, 1963. *Monte Carlo's opulent century.*

**The Casino Gambler's Guide** by Allan N. Wilson. Harper and Row, New York and Evanston, 1971.

**Challenge to Chance** by E. Lenox Figgis. Arco Publications Ltd., London, 1957.

**Gambling** by Alan Wykes. Aldus Books Ltd., London, 1964.

**The Green Felt Jungle** by Ed Reid and Ovid Demaris. Trident Press, New York, 1963. *The Las Vegas story.*

**Hell and Hazard** by Henry Blyth. Weidenfeld and Nicolson, London, 1969. *William Crockford versus the Gentlemen of England.*

**The Ladbrokes Story** by Richard Kaye. Pelham Books, 1969.

**None But the Rich** by Charles Graves. Cassell, London, 1963. *The life and times of the Greek Syndicate.*

**Oswald Jacoby on Gambling.** Hart Publishing Co., Inc., New York, 1963.

**Scarne's Complete Guide to Gambling** by John Scarne. Simon and Schuster, New York, 1961.

124